LEARN TO
DRIVE
IN 10 EASY STAGES

LEARN TO
DRIVE
IN 10 EASY STAGES

NIGEL & MARGARET STACEY

Illustrated by Andy Rice

KOGAN PAGE

Copyright © Nigel Stacey, Margaret Stacey, Andrew Rice 1987

First published in Great Britain in 1987
by Kogan Page Ltd, 120 Pentonville Road, London N1 9JN

Reprinted 1987, 1988 (twice), 1989
Revised edition published 1990
Reprinted 1991, 1992

British Library Cataloguing in Publication Data
Stacey, Nigel
    Learn to Drive in ten easy stages
    1. Automobile Driving
    I. Title   II. Stacey, Margaret, *1946–*
    629.28'32   TL152.5

ISBN 1-85091-137-1

Printed and bound in Great Britain by
BAS Printers Limited, Over Wallop, Hampshire

Nigel Stacey: was also the author of 'Running Your Own Driving School' and 'The Driving Instructor's Handbook' (now approved and recommended by the Department of Transport as reading material for driving instructors), both published by Kogan Page. Nigel's life's work lay in the training of hundreds of new drivers and driving instructors under his 'Autodriva' system. His influence in the driver training industry is still significant and he is a sad loss to those who recognised his professional expertise and valued him as a colleague and friend. Nigel's work and published materials benefited from contributions from his wife, *Margaret Stacey* who continues to operate under the 'Autodriva' name and to revise and update these publications since Nigel's untimely death. This work is based upon the Autodriva principles and is of benefit as a supplement to professional tuition.

Contents

Introduction

This guide has been produced to provide provisional licence holders with a comprehensive course in learning to drive. It shows them what to expect from lessons and includes everything they need to know to pass their driving test. Emphasis throughout is on reducing the high risk of accidents for newly qualified drivers.

Learning to drive, and pass the test, is often a haphazard, superficial and time-consuming process. Trying to study aspects of the Highway Code which are unrelated to in-car practice is ineffective, frustrating and time wasting.

This systematic step-by-step programme is designed to take the panic and confusion out of practice and enable learners to reduce the overall cost of lessons through more effective practice and use of their time. The special Highway Code study programmes add more meaning to, and promote the application of, rules.

The lesson guides include common-sense advice on everything from choosing a school to how to change a wheel and they allow learners to plan and pace themselves according to their own natural aptitude and ability.

The illustrations help drivers to recognise risk sooner, predict potential danger and avoid conflict with less able drivers taught merely to pass the test. During field trials the programme has achieved driving test pass rates of over double the national average. Consequently its structure was adopted by the National Joint Council of Approved Driving Instructors as a teaching model for both new drivers and trainee instructors. For further information about advanced driving and instructor training courses contact the authors at AUTODRIVA, The Mount, 53 Heanor Road, Ilkeston, Derbyshire DE7 8DY, telephone 0602 3244999.

How to Use the Guide

The guide contains ten step-by-step lessons. Keep to the lesson sequence and make sure you have mastered all the points before you move on to the next one.

Read the introduction to the lesson and learn the Highway Code rules listed

Follow the instructions found in each introduction and learn the Highway Code rules as directed.

Learn the key points of the lesson

Each lesson identifies the key learning points. Read through it and think carefully about the points covered. Make sure you understand these before practising in the car.

Complete the checkpoint

Test your knowledge before practising in the car by completing the checkpoint. Tick the most appropriate answers in pencil and match them against those given at the foot of the page.

In-car lessons and practice

Each lesson shows you what to do in the car. Be sure to get enough practice on all the points covered.

Only move on to the next lesson when you feel confident you have mastered them all.

Limit the initial time you spend practising something new to about 10 to 15 minutes, then take a three- or four-minute break. Use this time to discuss your performance and then practise it again.

Revise at the start of each lesson

At the beginning of each practice period you should spend a few minutes going over what you did on your last lesson or practice session.

Special revision chart

A revision chart, linked to the Department of Transport driving test syllabus, can be found on pages 145-6. Use this to identify areas of weakness and organise your revision. The page references will give you rapid access to the text you need to revise the most.

Thousands of instructors throughout the UK use a special appointment card and progress record. These give you instant feedback on how you are progressing and which areas you need to revise. Match the points your instructor has recorded on your card to those on the chart.

Before You Drive

Introduction

Before starting this lesson you should read about how to use the guide on page 8.

This first lesson tells you what to look for in a driving school and gives you some advice about practice with friends and relatives. It also covers a few common-sense, but none the less important, things which you need to know before driving on the road.

Learn the Highway Code rules we have listed below before working through the main part of the lesson.

Rules	26-27	Vehicle condition, safety and 'L' plates.
Rules	29-33	Health, eyesight and tinted optical equipment.
Rule	34	Alcohol.
Rules	35-37	Seat belts.
Rule	119	Operation and cleanliness of lights.
Rule	148	Animals in your car.

After learning the Highway Code rules, work through the lesson. When you have done this, complete the checkpoint at the end of the chapter by selecting an answer using a pencil so that you can rub out any incorrect ones.

Match your answers with those given at the foot of the page. Rub out any wrong ones and revise that particular part of the lesson. Try those questions again until you have got them all correct. Do not cheat!

Choosing a driving school

Make sure that you choose a Department of Transport Approved Driving Instructor by asking to see the green certificate bearing his or her photograph. This should be on display in the windscreen of the car. Some self-employed instructors may not be qualified. Others working for larger multi-car schools may be trainees who have not yet passed the qualifying examinations. These trainees should display a red certificate in the car. You can make doubly sure an instructor is competent by choosing one who is a National Joint Council Tutor, holds the Diploma in Driving Instruction, or is RAC Registered.

Do not be fooled by the strings of initials after the names of some instructors. These often refer to organisations which have no expertise in training new drivers or national instructor associations which accept unqualified and unlicensed instructors simply to obtain the membership fee.

The wrong choice may mean failed tests, more lessons and extra costs.

Ask around and go to the instructor with the most *first-time* passes. Find one who provides simple step-by-step training like that outlined in this guide, and who gives a written lesson-by-lesson record of appointments and of your progress.

Planning a course of lessons

Quality varies more than price, so when you are comparing the cost per lesson think about how many lessons you may need. For example, 30 lessons at £12 each is £90 less than 50 at £9! Remember too that some prices quoted may be per hour while others may be for 45-minute lessons or less. Avoid instructors who call for clients with the previous one in the car. You may waste between 15 and 40 minutes of lesson time driving the previous client home and picking the next one up, which increases your costs even more! The total lessons needed will vary according to age, aptitude and the amount of practice you get. Most people need between one to one and a half lessons for each year of their age. You will normally need fewer lessons overall if you take two or three a week.

If you need to learn fairly quickly, it is normally better to spread lessons over four or five weeks than to cram them into one or two weeks on an intensive *group* course. Before going on such a course find out how many learners are in the car together, how many hours driving you get and the amount of time spent in the classroom.

Practising with friends and relatives

It is best to have at least a few lessons with a school before practising with friends or relatives. If you are practising privately, your supervisor must be over 21 and must have held a full driving licence for three years. Not all drivers make good instructors and if you learn bad habits at the start, they can stay with you for a long time. They can also ruin your confidence by leading you into situations you cannot deal with. Close relatives are often too personally involved and tend to get over-anxious and agitated. If they 'tell you off' unjustly, keep cool and try to 'bite your lip'. Responding angrily only leads to further argument.

brake. Learning is no excuse for breaking the law and careless driving could result in a disqualification for both of you. Make sure you can stop quickly before driving in traffic and if you really feel you cannot cope get your supervisor to take over.

Work through the guide with your supervisor before setting off and make sure that you both understand what to do. If you are not quite sure, ask for further explanation. If you find something really difficult and get stuck on it, try something new for a while and then go back to it later.

Avoid driving in fog and heavy snow during your

Before practising privately, get an extra rear view suction mirror fitted to the windscreen for your supervisor. Remember the vehicle does not have dual-controls so do not try to do too much too soon. Keep out of trouble by selecting routes which you can cope with. Supervisors can help you by thinking ahead and giving clear instructions in time for you to carry them out. If things do get out of hand they should be prepared to compensate, for example, with steering corrections or by applying the hand-

first few lessons. There are too many other new things for you to think about. Although Sunday practice may be quite useful in the intermediate and early stages of learning, it usually fails to provide the kind of conditions you will experience during the test. Most later lessons should be in busier conditions and you should try to gain some experience of driving in the dark before taking the test. During the last few weeks before the test, practice should be in busy daylight hours.

Making it legal to drive

The minimum age for driving a small passenger or goods vehicle is normally 17. If you are in receipt of a mobility allowance the minimum age is 16. You can apply for the licence up to two months before you want it to commence. A provisional licence only allows you to drive motor cars and small vans under the supervision of a qualified driver or Department of Transport Approved Driving Instructor.

Make sure any vehicle you intend driving is taxed. You can do this by checking the expiry date on the windscreen tax disc. Also check the vehicle is properly insured for you to drive and that it covers you for learning.

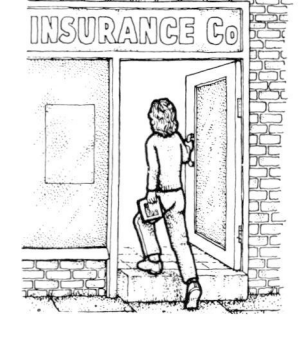 

If you are taking medicines or drugs you should ask your doctor how they will affect your driving.

Alcohol is a drug which impairs the perception of danger. It makes people believe they can achieve the impossible and blurs their judgement of speed and distance. Even small amounts of alcohol will slow your reactions and it is a major cause of road accidents. If you drink heavily the night before a lesson, the amount of alcohol in your body may still be exceeding the legal limit in the morning.

If the vehicle you are learning in is over three years old it must undergo an annual MOT Test. Check the test certificate. Although this shows it passed the MOT on the day, it does not mean the vehicle is still roadworthy.

Before getting into a car, have a look round for flat or badly worn tyres. Check that the indicators and lights work before you drive away.

Scratched or dirty windows make driving tiring and more difficult. Glare from bright sunlight and the headlights of other cars can become painful to the eyes. Use water and a soft cloth or leather to wash windows inside and out. Also clean the mirrors and lights.

Condensation can also restrict your vision, particularly in cold or damp weather. Use the demister, the rear screen heater and a slightly open window to clear condensation and prevent it from reforming.

How to reduce distractions while learning

It is a good idea to visit the toilet before a lesson as any discomfort affects concentration. Get ready in plenty of time so you can spend a few minutes relaxing. This will help you to collect your thoughts and mentally prepare yourself for the lesson. You should try to avoid arguments because they will put you in the wrong frame of mind for both driving and learning. Display 'L' plates so they can be clearly seen from the front and rear. The bumper is usually the best place to put them. You must not restrict your view of the road in front or behind. Do not put 'L' plates in the windows and take down any stickers or toy mascots which might restrict your view.

It is not normally a good idea to carry extra passengers during your first few lessons. If you do, always try to organise them so that they get in from the footpath side and sit them where they do not restrict your view in the mirror.

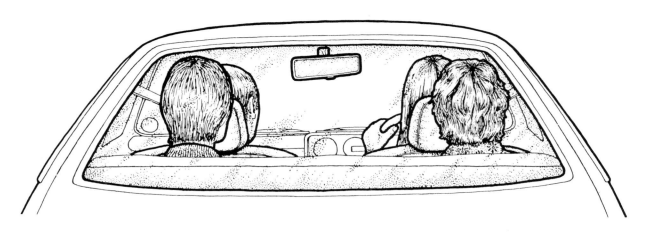

How to reduce distractions while driving

Children can get bored quite quickly and may make it difficult for you to concentrate properly on driving. If you must have them in the car when practising make sure that they are restrained and kept under control.

Make sure there is nothing on the floor that is likely to roll around such as a child's ball. Apart from being a distraction, if an aerosol can or other object rolls under the pedals it may prevent the brakes from being applied.

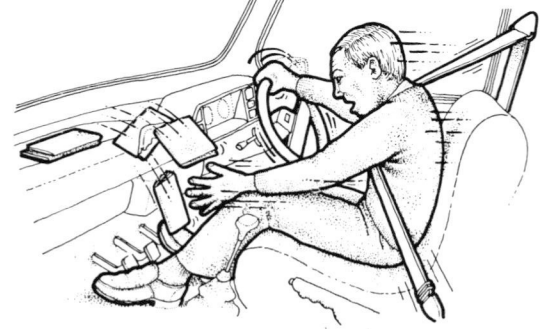

Before driving away, look round for loose articles which might distract you. Tidy up maps, papers or other things lying around. If they fall about when accelerating, slowing down or cornering they could distract you and cause an accident.

The concentration needed to drive can be quite tiring and you will need plenty of fresh air in the car to help you to stay alert. During cold weather you should keep the in-car temperature comfortable, but not too warm.

Getting ready for your first lesson

Wear light, comfortable and loose fitting clothes. Heavy coats are unnecessary with modern car heating systems. Also they may restrict your arm action on the steering wheel and make it difficult to turn. Avoid any tight fitting clothes which may restrict your body movements.

Make sure that you can read a modern number plate with the 3⅛ inch high symbols from at least 67 feet. If you need glasses to do this you must also wear them for driving.

Wear flat shoes for driving which have an enclosed or covered heel. Heavy boots and fashion shoes are normally unsuitable and make it awkward to control the pedals.

Stage 1

Checkpoint

1. When booking lessons should you:
   [a] choose the cheapest school?
   [b] ask to see the instructor's certificate?

2. After applying for your first provisional licence you:
   [a] can drive straight away.
   [b] must wait to receive it before driving.

3. The minimum age for driving a motor car is:
   [a] usually 16 years old.
   [b] normally 17 years old.

4. Before driving should you make sure the:
   [a] mirrors and windscreen are clean?
   [b] lights and indicators work?
   [c] both [a] and [b]?

5. Before driving, should you make sure you can:
   [a] read a number plate at 67 feet?
   [b] read a number plate at 67 yards?

6. Passengers should get in from the:
   [a] off-side.
   [b] footpath side.

7. If you are taking medicines should you:
   [a] ask your doctor if you can drive?
   [b] decide yourself if you can drive?

8. Cars used for lessons and practice must be:
   [a] taxed and insured.
   [b] roadworthy.
   [c] both [a] and [b].

9. Provisional licence holders must:
   [a] display 'L' plates in the windows.
   [b] display 'L' plates clearly front and rear.

10. Your vehicle should display:
    [a] a valid tax disc.
    [b] an MOT test certificate.
    [c] an insurance certificate.

11. An MOT certificate is normally needed if your car is over:
    [a] one year old.
    [b] two years old.
    [c] three years old.

12. Small children should be:
    [a] carried only in the rear of a car.
    [b] kept under control.
    [c] both [a] and [b].

13. Loose papers should be:
    [a] kept in the glove compartment.
    [b] kept on the rear window ledge.
    [c] put on the floor in the rear.

14. Window stickers and toy mascots:
    [a] may restrict the driver's view.
    [b] may hide danger.
    [c] both [a] and [b].

15. Loose articles falling about in a car:
    [a] can distract the driver.
    [b] cause accidents.
    [c] both [a] and [b].

16. Tinted windows improve vision:
    [a] at night.
    [b] in the daytime.
    [c] neither [a] nor [b].

17. Tinted glasses should not be used:
    [a] in poor day time visibility.
    [b] at night.
    [c] both [a] and [b].

Checkpoint answers

1. [b]   2. [b]   3. [b]   4. [c]   5. [a]   6. [b]
7. [a]   8. [c]   9. [b]   10. [a]   11. [c]   12. [c]
13. [a]   14. [c]   15. [c]   16. [c]   17. [c]

Get to Know Your Car

First you should learn Highway Code Rules 128 and 129.

This lesson will give you a chance to get the feel of the controls and practise some simple exercises before moving away.

Make sure that you understand and can carry out the following instructions before starting Lesson 3 or attempting to move off:

The instruction	What it means
Handbrake ready.	Put your hand on to the handbrake ready to release it.
Set the gas.	Press the accelerator gently to increase the engine speed to a fast tickover ready for moving off.
Find the holding point.	Allow the clutch pedal to come up until you hear the engine slow down a little. Keep your foot still as soon as you hear the engine note change. This is often called the biting point.
Cover the clutch.	Place your left foot over the clutch pedal without touching it.
Cover the brake.	Place your right foot over the brake pedal without pressing it.

After learning the Highway Code rules and instructions listed above, work through the lesson and complete the checkpoint before going out in the car.

As you work through the lesson you will find other instructions which you must practise before moving away. They are not listed because they are spoken in plain everyday English and need no explanation, for example, 'move the gear lever into 1st' or 'take the handbrake off'.

Complete the checkpoint by ticking the most appropriate answer. Use pencil so that you can rub out any incorrect ones. Match your answers with those given at the foot of the page. Rub out any incorrect answers and revise that particular part of the lesson. Answer those questions again until you get them all correct. Do not cheat!

Stage 2

Getting into the 'cockpit drill' habit

1. Doors

Opening a car door carelessly can put you in danger. It may force others to brake or swerve and could cause an accident.

Get in as quickly as you can, close the door and listen to make sure that any passengers have closed theirs. A door not shut properly will rattle and may fly open as you drive along.

Also check the handbrake is firmly on.

DOORS
CHECKED

2. Seat

Adjust the seat and get comfortable. Sit up with your bottom well back in the seat and make sure you can see clearly ahead. If you need more height use a cushion.

To test the seat position, push the pedal on the far left (the clutch) down to the floor. You should be able to do this without stretching. Do not get too close or you may find it awkward to let the pedal up and control the clutch.

Hold the wheel in this position. Your arms should be slightly bent and your elbows clear of your body. Test to see if you can move your hands freely from the top of the wheel to the bottom. If you find this awkward, you could be sitting too close and may have to readjust the seat.

SEAT
CHECKED

3. Mirrors

Use the mirror well before you signal and change speed or direction. Adjust it so that you can see clearly to the rear with the minimum of head movement. Hold it as shown and keep your fingers off the glass. Line up the top edge of the mirror along the top edge of the rear window. Line up the offside edge (driver's side) of the rear window down its right side.

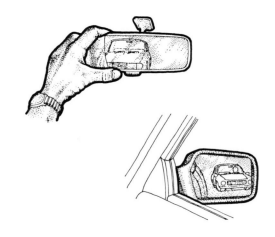

Adjust the door mirrors to reduce the blind areas at your sides. Use these before you move off, change lanes or turn.

MIRRORS

CHECKED

4. Seatbelts

Adjust and fasten your seatbelt and make sure that passengers are wearing theirs.

Small children must be carried in the rear seats only and must be fastened securely in approved harnesses or child seats. Switch the child 'safety' door locks on so that they cannot be opened from inside.

SEATBELTS

CHECKED

How to start the engine

Before you start the engine check that the handbrake ▶
(parking brake) is on and the gear lever in neutral.
Failure to do this may result in the car lurching away
when you operate the starter. The starter or ignition
switch is normally on or near the steering column
and usually combines an anti-theft steering lock.

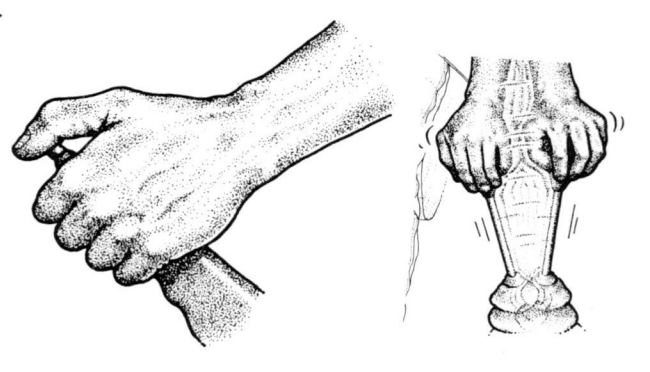

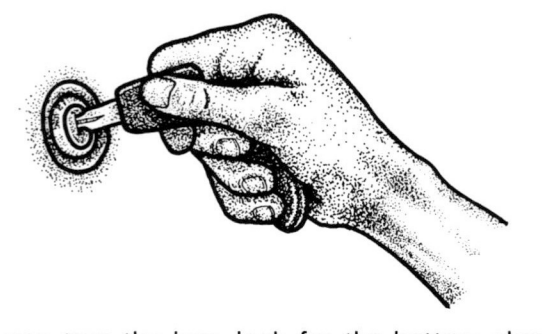

▲
As you turn the key, look for the battery charging
and oil pressure warning lights. Check these go out
when the engine starts.

   Turn the key gently to operate the starter; when
the engine starts let it go. To stop the engine turn the
key back to its original position.

If the engine will not start, press the accelerator (the
pedal on the right) slightly and try again. Do not
pump the pedal, though, as this can flood the engine
and make starting difficult.
▼

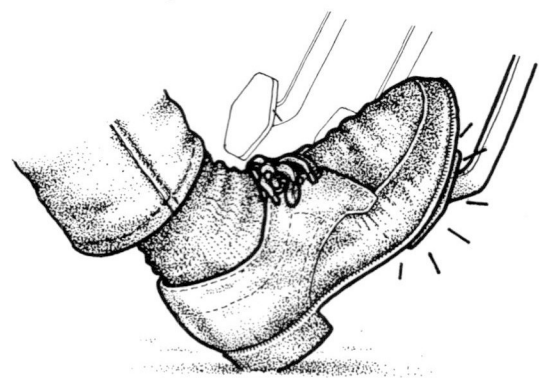

◀ To start a cold engine, you may need the choke to
increase the fuel flow. But remember to push it in
again as soon as the engine is warm.

When to use the handbrake

The handbrake is used to secure the car when ▶ parked or stationary for more than a moment or so. It is also used to help you time moving off into gaps in the flow of traffic.

Except in the event of a main brake failure, it must only be applied when the car is stationary.

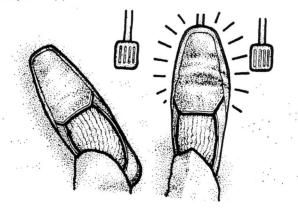

To release the handbrake put your hand on it, pull the lever up slightly and press the button. Keep the button pressed in while you push the handbrake down. ▼

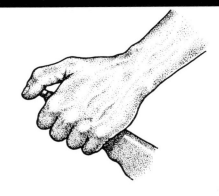

◀ You must be able to apply and release the handbrake quickly and without wearing the ratchet or looking down. Practise this before driving.

First, press your footbrake (the middle pedal) firmly with your right foot. This will hold the car still while you practise.

▲
To put it on again, press the button and, keeping it in, pull the lever up firmly. Release the button to lock the brake on.

How to steer and operate the controls

To steer accurately you must be able to operate the main controls without looking down at them. Looking down will result in your car wandering from side to side.

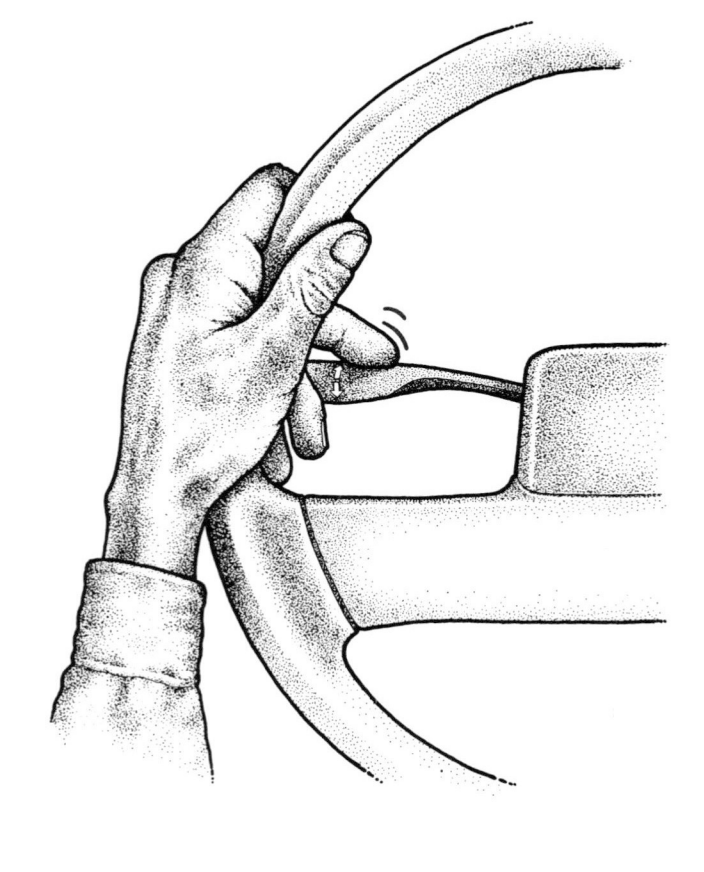

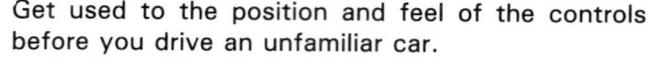

Get used to the position and feel of the controls before you drive an unfamiliar car.

The most frequently used switches, like the direction indicators, lights and windscreen wipers, are usually on the column just behind the steering wheel.

Practise using them with your fingertips, keeping your hands on the wheel.

Other important switches include the horn, windscreen washer and demisters. These can usually be left until you have mastered the main controls towards the end of Lesson 4.

How to hold the wheel and turn corners

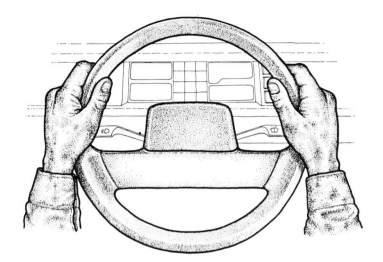

Hold the wheel in your fingers in this position. Fold your palms loosely over the rim and rest your thumbs lightly up the flat. Relax your shoulders and keep your arms free of your body.

Before removing one hand to change gear or use other controls, take a firmer grip with the other one. Try to keep two hands on the wheel when braking or cornering. Just before reaching a bend or corner slide the hand on the same side towards the top of the wheel ready to pull down and turn it.

For accurate positioning and steering it is more important for you to concentrate on where you want to go than on what your hands are doing.

On corners try to remember that the rear wheels will cut closer into the turn than the front of the car.

Using the gears

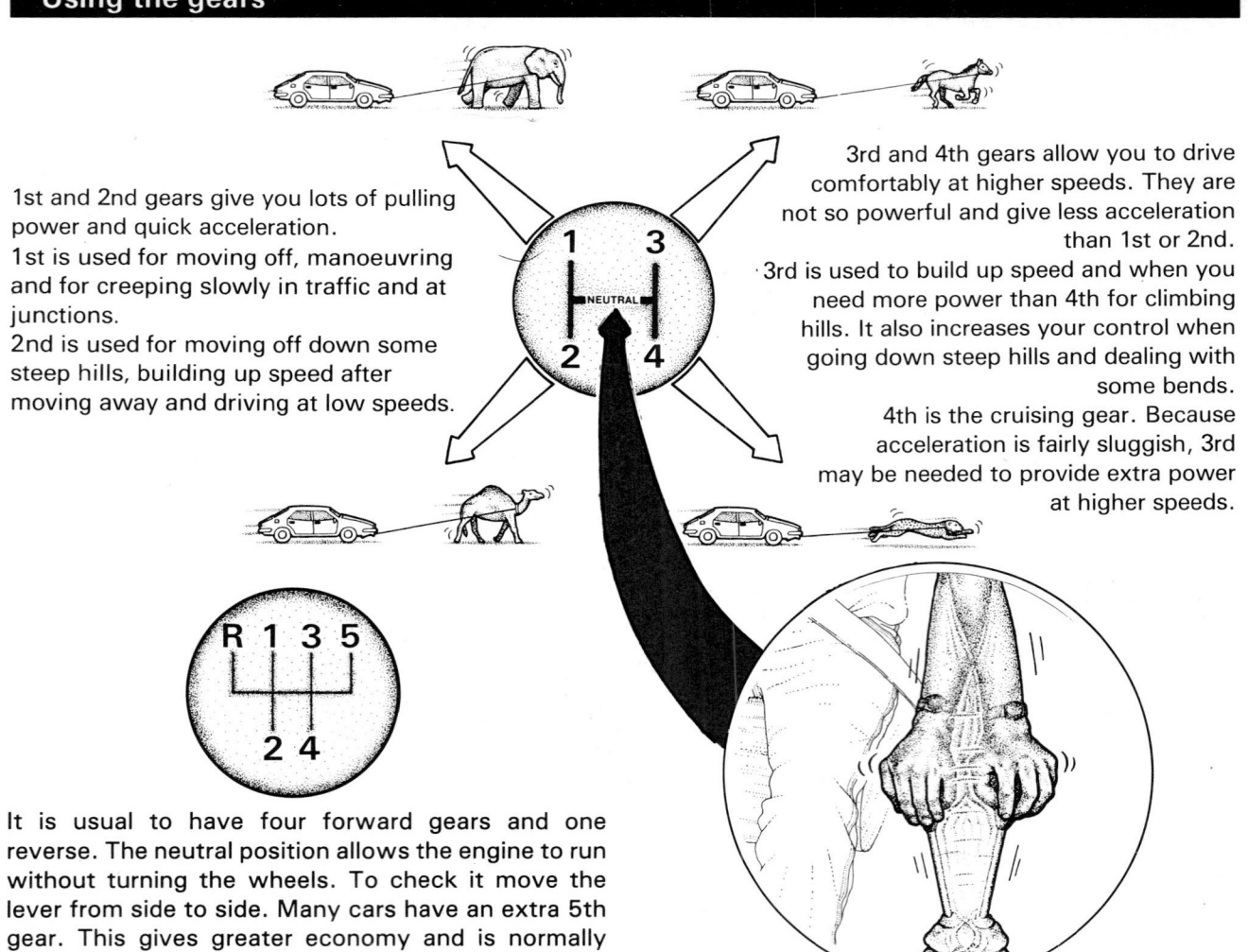

1st and 2nd gears give you lots of pulling power and quick acceleration.
1st is used for moving off, manoeuvring and for creeping slowly in traffic and at junctions.
2nd is used for moving off down some steep hills, building up speed after moving away and driving at low speeds.

3rd and 4th gears allow you to drive comfortably at higher speeds. They are not so powerful and give less acceleration than 1st or 2nd.
3rd is used to build up speed and when you need more power than 4th for climbing hills. It also increases your control when going down steep hills and dealing with some bends.
4th is the cruising gear. Because acceleration is fairly sluggish, 3rd may be needed to provide extra power at higher speeds.

It is usual to have four forward gears and one reverse. The neutral position allows the engine to run without turning the wheels. To check it move the lever from side to side. Many cars have an extra 5th gear. This gives greater economy and is normally only used on open roads.

How to change gear

From neutral to 1st

To practise finding 1st and 2nd gears, angle your palm and press the lever lightly away from you. Move it forwards to 1st gear then straight back to 2nd.

To select 3rd and 4th gears, angle the palm towards you. Move the lever gently from 2nd into 3rd and finally 4th.

Now move the lever back to 3rd, to 2nd and then to 1st. Keep practising until you have perfected these movements.

Finally, practise changing from 4th to 2nd and from 3rd to 1st.

Driving a car with an automatic transmission system

Learning to start, steer and stop is much easier when cars have automatic transmission. There is no clutch to worry about and once the initial selection has been made, all gear changes are carried out automatically. These are regulated by the vehicle speed and the pressure applied by the driver to the accelerator. Automatic transmission enables drivers to concentrate on the more important things such as planning ahead and steering. It is particulary helpful for older and disabled people. If you pass your test in an automatic vehicle, you get a licence to drive this type of car only.

The exercises set out in Lesson 4 are made much simpler but they should still be carried out. Your instructor will explain about the extra use of the handbrake and the different techniques used to control low speeds.

From 1st to 2nd   From 2nd to 3rd

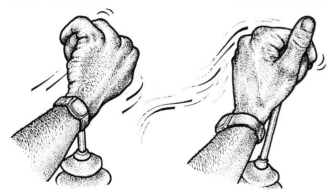

When driving, you must be able to change gear without looking down at the lever. You should practise this with the engine switched off and the clutch pressed down. Use a cupped palm to move the gear lever.

Stage
2

Using the clutch

To move off, change gear and stop, you must be able to use the clutch without looking down.

First, cover the clutch with your left foot and then press it down. This disconnects the engine from the gearbox. You will need to do this when selecting gears and just before stopping.

Next, let the pedal up smoothly. You will feel a powerful spring pushing your foot up.

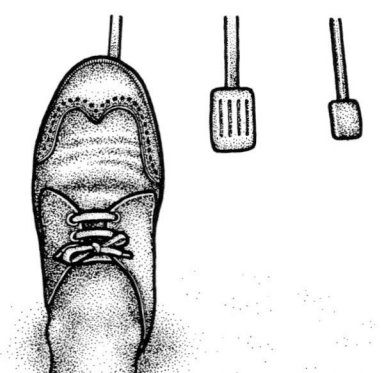

The Biting Range

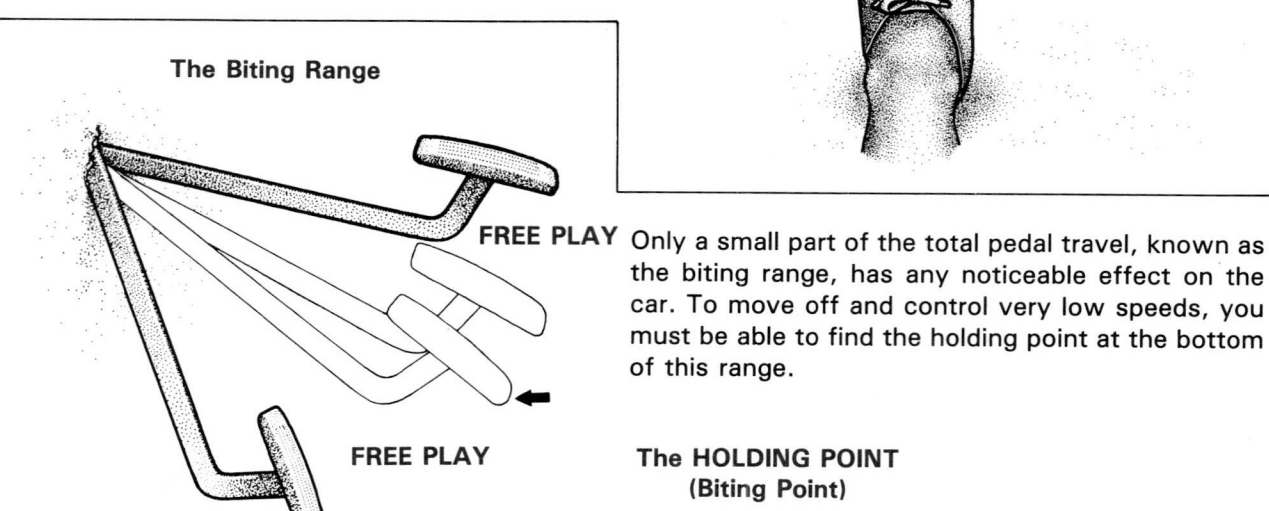

FREE PLAY

FREE PLAY

**The HOLDING POINT
(Biting Point)**

Only a small part of the total pedal travel, known as the biting range, has any noticeable effect on the car. To move off and control very low speeds, you must be able to find the holding point at the bottom of this range.

The clutch consists of two friction plates which you must bring together smoothly when moving off. To do this you must first find the holding point. This allows the plates to touch lightly without driving the car. When the handbrake is released with the clutch at the holding point, the car may creep away at a very low speed with what is known as a 'slipping clutch'.

How to find the holding (biting) point

To practise finding the holding point you should start the engine. Remember to make sure that the handbrake is on and the gear lever in neutral. When you have done this you should push the clutch down, select 1st gear and set the gas by squeezing the accelerator slightly until you hear a healthy purr, about half as fast again as the engine tickover speed.

Raise the clutch pedal slowly by bending your ankle. Keeping your heel on the floor will give you more support and positive clutch control. It may feel a little awkward at first, particularly if you have small feet or if you are driving a car with high pedals. Padding under the carpet may help to overcome these problems.

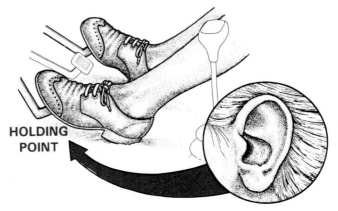

HOLDING POINT

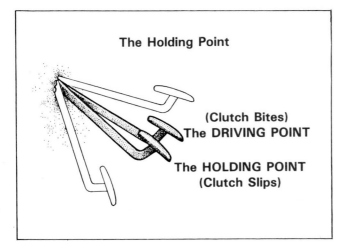

The Holding Point

(Clutch Bites)
The **DRIVING POINT**

The **HOLDING POINT**
(Clutch Slips)

As you raise the clutch, listen for a slight drop in the engine speed. When you hear or feel this, you have found the holding point and should keep the pedal still.

After keeping your foot still for a couple of seconds or so, push the pedal down again and release the accelerator.

Practise this until you can find the holding point fairly quickly every time.

Using the accelerator and footbrake

Position your right foot so that you can pivot easily between the accelerator and brake pedals. To do this, cover the brake pedal with your right foot. Without looking down or moving your heel, practise the pivot between the pedals.

Once you have found a comfortable position for your foot, get a feel for the brake pedal by pressing it lightly. The first pressure puts the stop light signals on. This lets those behind know you are braking. Once you have taken up the free play, the harder you press the more you will slow down.

Next, start the engine. Remember to make sure that the handbrake is on and the gear lever in neutral.

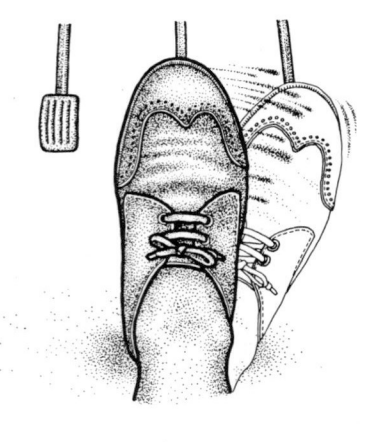

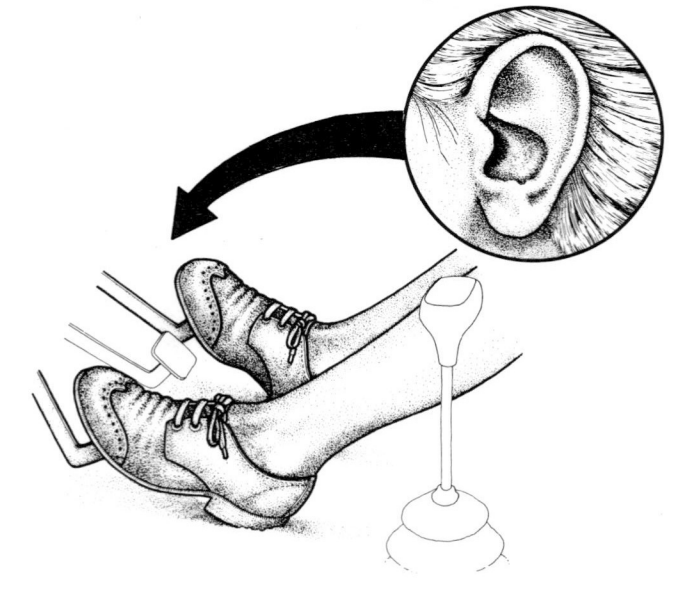

Listen to the engine tickover speed and squeeze the accelerator slowly until you hear a healthy purr which should be about half as fast again. This is called setting the gas and you do it before moving off. You must practise this until you get it just right every time.

After moving off, you will notice that the car will respond quicker to pressure on the accelerator when you are in the lower gears. Releasing pressure gives a slowing effect which is also more pronounced in 1st and 2nd gears.

Checkpoint

1. The cockpit drill sequence is:

    [a] doors, seat, mirror, seatbelt.
    [b] doors, mirror, seat, seatbelt.

2. Seatbelts reduce:

    [a] accidents by 50 per cent.
    [b] risk of injury or death by 50 per cent.

3. The most frequently used switches are:

    [a] positioned near the steering wheel.
    [b] positioned on the dashboard.
    [c] positioned on the centre console.

4. The right foot pivots between:

    [a] clutch and brake pedals.
    [b] clutch and accelerator pedals.
    [c] accelerator and brake pedals.

5. The left foot operates:

    [a] the brake and clutch.
    [b] the clutch.
    [c] the brake.

6. To steer should you concentrate mostly:

    [a] on what your hands are doing?
    [b] on where you want to go?

7. Before starting the engine should you:

    [a] check the parking brake is on?
    [b] check the gear lever is in neutral?
    [c] both [a] and [b].

8. Starting the engine while in gear may:

    [a] cause the car to lurch forwards.
    [b] damage the handbrake.

9. The clutch:

    [a] transmits engine power to the gearbox.
    [b] controls the speed of the engine.

10. Side mirrors:

    [a] reduce blind spots.
    [b] compensate completely for blind spots.

11. The choke is used to start the engine:

    [a] when hot.
    [b] when cold.

12. Two hands should be on the steering wheel:

    [a] when braking.
    [b] when cornering.
    [c] both [a] and [b].

13. Direction indicators can normally be:

    [a] operated without releasing the wheel.
    [b] operated with either hand.

14. The handbrake should be applied:

    [a] the instant a car stops.
    [b] when stopped for more than a second or so.

15. In neutral, the engine is:

    [a] disconnected from the wheels.
    [b] connected to the wheels.

16. 1st is the:

    [a] least powerful gear.
    [b] most economical gear.
    [c] most powerful gear.

Checkpoint answers

1. [a]   2. [b]   3. [a]   4. [c]   5. [b]   6. [b]

7. [c]   8. [a]   9. [a]   10. [a]   11. [b]   12. [c]

13. [a]   14. [b]   15. [a]   16. [c]

Starting to Drive

Introduction

Make sure you have mastered all the points and practised the exercises in Lesson 2 before starting this one. During this lesson you will be learning to move off, change gear, steer and stop.

It is better to learn the points covered in this lesson with a Department of Transport Approved Instructor before practising with others. A professional instructor will drive you to a fairly straight road in a quiet area to start. Housing estates or roads with lots of junctions and parked cars are unsuitable for your first practice.

An experienced instructor will talk you, step by step, through each skill until you can manage on your own. Listen carefully for any directions to turn, and concentrate on what your instructor is telling you to do. Try to avoid talking while you are moving unless you need to ask a specific question.

Professional instructors normally give you plenty of warning about turns, but when practising with friends or relatives you may find yourself short of time. If you do, you should tell them and ask for more warning. Although it is polite to look at people when they are talking to you, do not do it when you are driving. Try to keep your eyes on the road ahead.

Directions should be given clearly thus:

1. *I want you to take the next road on the left.*
2. *Take the second road on the right; this is the first.*
3. *At the end of the road turn left.*
4. *At the roundabout take the road leading off to the right. That is the third exit.*

Before going out to practise you should first learn the Highway Code rules listed below:

Rules	42-43	Moving off and the normal driving position.
Rules	124-125	Parking.
Rule	127	Parking areas.
Rule	129	Parking close to the kerb.

After reading the instructions and learning the Highway Code rules, work through the lesson and complete the checkpoint before going out in the car. Match your answers with those given at the foot of the page. Rub out any wrong ones and revise that particular part of the lesson.

Stage

3

How to move off

You should normally use 1st gear for moving off except when pulling away down a steep hill.

Get ready to move: first look to the front and in the mirrors for traffic and pedestrians and then get ready to move.

To prepare to move, push the clutch down and select 1st gear. Set the gas and get the handbrake ready. Find the holding point and keep the clutch still.

Check it is safe to move: check it is safe to go by looking in the interior and door mirrors. To be 100 per cent sure, look round for other road users in your blind spots. Be prepared to wait. Decide if you need to signal. You should give a signal if it will help to warn or inform others that you are moving away.

To move away: you can time the precise moment for moving off with the release of the handbrake. Decide to do this only when you are sure it is safe. It should allow the car to creep forwards. If it does not, let the clutch up a little more.

To increase speed, press the accelerator gently and, once the car is moving, start easing the clutch up slowly. Continue to press the accelerator gently as you raise the clutch smoothly to the top.

You will need to change into 2nd gear soon after moving off.

How to change gear

1st gear provided the power you needed for pulling the car away. As soon as you have done this, you will need to change into 2nd gear. This will enable you to accelerate from the low speed. Remember, when selecting 1st and 2nd gears, to angle your palm away from you.

Preparing to change (from 1st to 2nd): grip the wheel a little more firmly with your right hand and cover the clutch ready to press it down.

Cup your left palm and place it on to the gear lever angled away from you.

Keep your eyes on the road and try to find the gear lever without looking down.

▼

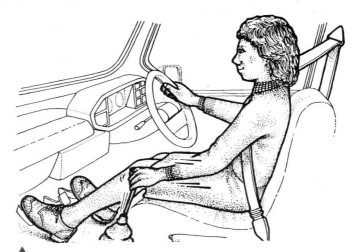

▲

To change gear (from 1st to 2nd): push the clutch down quickly and take your foot off the gas simultaneously. At the same time use gentle pressure to move the gear lever from 1st to 2nd.

Raise the clutch smoothly to the top and then press the accelerator gently to increase the engine speed and drive the car.

Return your hand to the wheel.

After accelerating in 2nd gear to about 20mph or so, change to 3rd. Use this to build up to about 30mph or so, and then change into 4th. For 3rd and 4th gears, remember to angle your palm towards you.

It is inadvisable to drive for prolonged periods with the clutch covered. As soon as you get into 4th gear, ▶ place your left foot on the floor or put it to the left of the pedal.

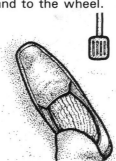

How to steer and judge your driving position

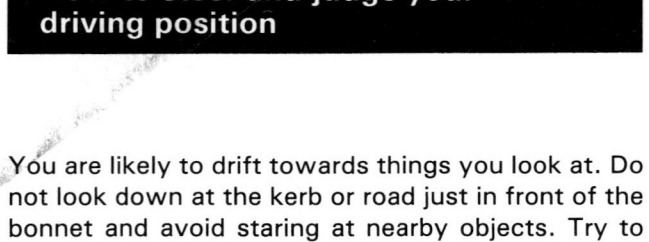

You are likely to drift towards things you look at. Do not look down at the kerb or road just in front of the bonnet and avoid staring at nearby objects. Try to drive about two or three feet out from the kerb and look to where you want to go. Plan your course well ahead by memorising the position of any obstructions. Rely on your side vision to sense your position in the road and to judge the clearance you are leaving between your car and parked vehicles.

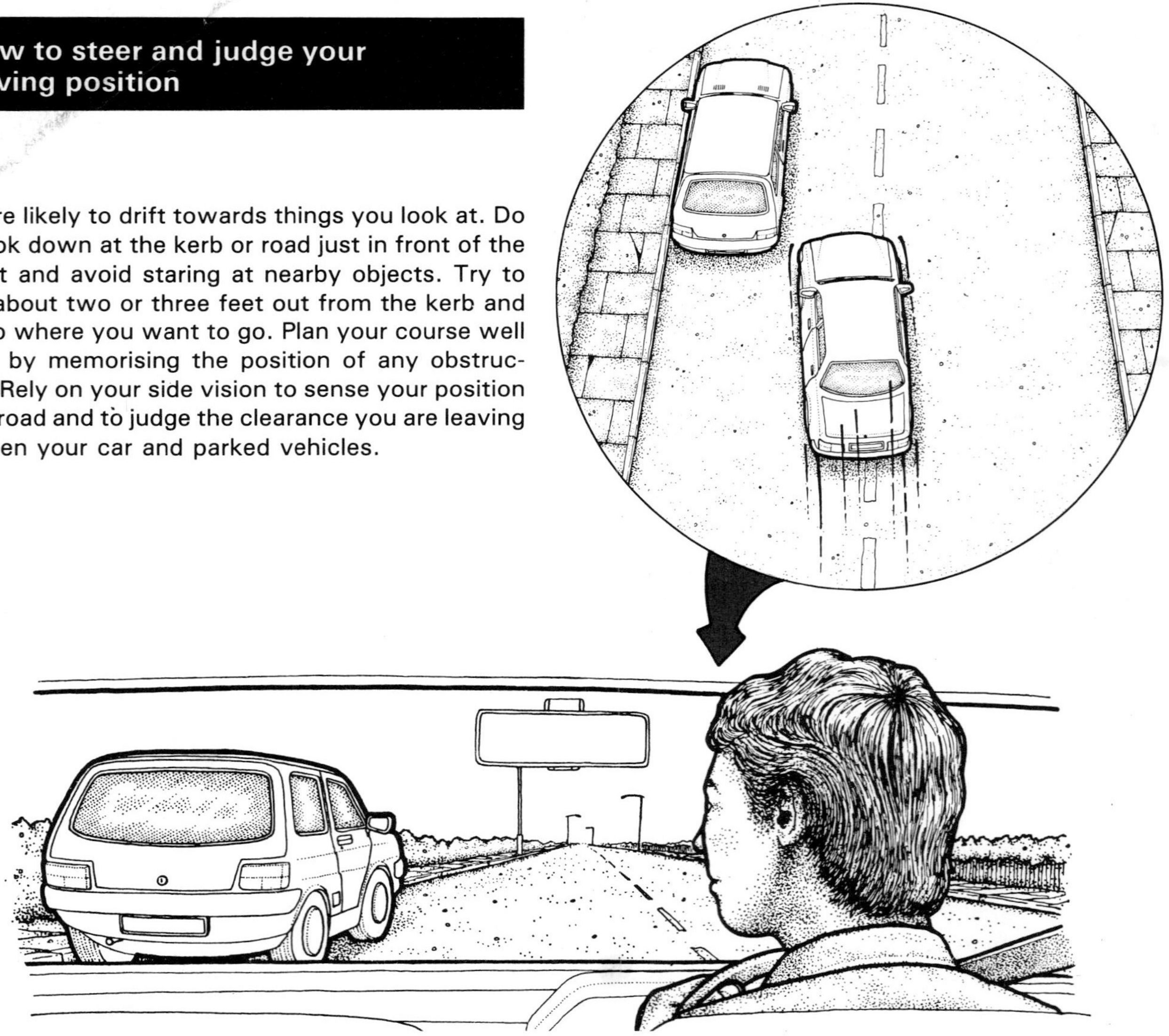

How to steer and drive at a safe speed

Look into the distance for road signs or obstructions and be prepared to slow down well before reaching any bends, junctions or traffic hold-ups.

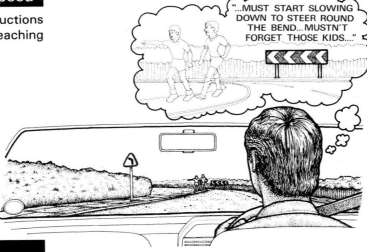

How to stop within the distance you can see to be clear

Look, and be ready to slow down, for other road users who might move into the road or turn across your path. Watch out for people and vehicles moving out from behind obstructions.

Stage

3

The mirror-signal-manoeuvre routine

It is never too soon for you to start getting into the mirror-signal-manoeuvre habit.

Using the mirror

You should check your mirror well before signalling and making changes in your speed or direction. You should check it before moving off and accelerating, before pulling out to pass parked cars, overtaking or positioning to turn and before slowing down or stopping.

Giving signals

You should give a signal if it will help to warn or inform any other road user of your intentions. The signals you will mostly be concerned with at this stage are the stop light signals and the direction indicators. The red stop light signals at the rear of your car will come on automatically when you press the footbrake. They tell people behind you that you are slowing down. If you see these lights on a vehicle ahead you should check your mirror and start easing off the accelerator in preparation for braking. Direction indicators flash at both the front and rear of your car to let others know when you want to change direction or stop. Signals should normally be given early so that other people have plenty of time to see them.

Making a manoeuvre

'Manoeuvre' is used to describe any change which you make in your position or speed. It also involves continually looking and assessing what is happening around you.

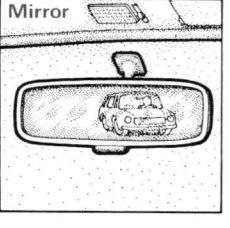
Mirror

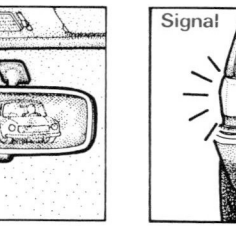
Signal

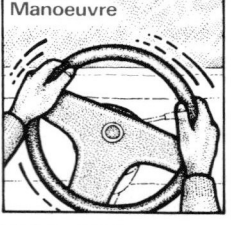
Manoeuvre

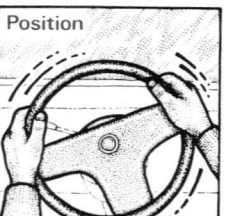
Position

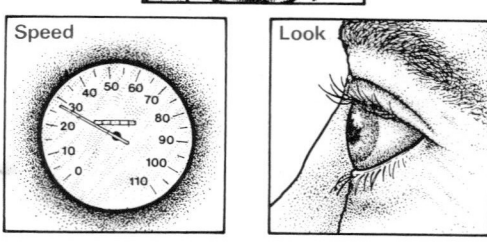
Speed

Look

Stopping and parking

Try to park well away from bends, junctions and hilltops. These are all places where the driver's view is already restricted.

A parked vehicle will increase the danger by forcing others on to the wrong side of the road where approaching traffic cannot be seen.

Find a straight part of the road and stop as close to the kerb as you can without bumping it. Carry out the mirror-signal-manoeuvre routine. First check for traffic coming up behind and, if necessary, signal to tell others what you are doing.

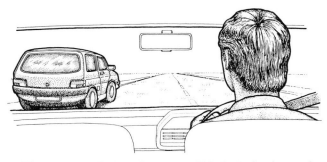

The secret of stopping smoothly is to brake early. Keep both hands on the wheel until the car comes to a stop. Brake gently at first, gradually building up into a firm pressure until you feel the car slowing down slightly more than you think is necessary. Gradually ease some pressure from the brake to let the car roll a little further.

Remember to push the clutch down just before you stop and keep it down until you have applied the handbrake and put the gear lever into neutral. Finally, rest your feet and switch the engine off.

Before opening the door to get out of the car, look round for people who may be hidden in the blind spot.

Stage 3

Checkpoint

1. To move off, should you:
   [a] push the clutch down and then select 1st?
   [b] set the engine speed and then select 1st?

2. Set the gas refers to:
   [a] the clutch and 'biting range'.
   [b] the accelerator and engine speed.

3. To find the holding point, should you:
   [a] listen to the engine speed?
   [b] look at your feet?

4. To control the clutch, it helps to:
   [a] keep your heel on the floor.
   [b] find the 'holding point', first.
   [c] both [a] and [b].

5. Before moving off, should you:
   [a] check the interior mirror?
   [b] check the door mirror?
   [c] both [a] and [b]?

6. Also, before moving off, should you:
   [a] check your mirrors?
   [b] look round over your shoulder?
   [c] both [a] and [b]

7. When preparing to change gear, should you:
   [a] get your hand on to the gear lever?
   [b] cover the clutch?
   [c] both [a] and [b]?

8. To move the gear lever, should you:
   [a] use a cupped palm?
   [b] grip the lever tightly?

9. To steer accurately, should you look:
   [a] well ahead?
   [b] at the kerb just ahead of the bonnet?
   [c] at the centre road markings?

10. In normal driving, should you steer:
    [a] about 3 feet out from the kerb?
    [b] as close to the kerb as you can?
    [c] about 1 foot out from the kerb?

11. Parking near bends and hill crests:
    [a] puts other road users at risk.
    [b] may cause a head-on collision.
    [c] both [a] and [b].

12. The correct sequence is:
    [a] signal, manoeuvre, mirror.
    [b] mirror, signal, manoeuvre.
    [c] signal, mirror, manoeuvre.

13. Stop lights switch on automatically when:
    [a] direction indicators are used.
    [b] the footbrake is pressed.

14. To stop smoothly and accurately, you should:
    [a] brake early.
    [b] keep both hands on the wheel.
    [c] both [a] and [b].

15. Before leaving your vehicle, you must:
    [a] switch the engine off.
    [b] set the parking brake.
    [c] both [a] and [b].

16. The correct sequence for braking is:
    [a] light – hard.
    [b] light – firm – light.

Checkpoint answers

1. [a] 2. [b] 3. [a] 4. [c] 5. [c] 6. [c]
7. [c] 8. [a] 9. [a] 10. [a] 11. [c] 12. [b]
13. [b] 14. [c] 15. [c] 16. [b].

Systematic Driving Practice

Introduction

So far your instructor has been telling you what to do and when to do it. This helps you to get things right first time and builds up your confidence. Lesson 4 consists of a series of structured exercises designed to get you doing more for yourself. Practise each step of each exercise separately until you completely master it.

When you can perform all the exercises in this lesson you can also start practising the exercises described in Lesson 6.

A professional instructor will always keep a look-out for other road users. This allows you to practise the exercises in safety. If you are learning with friends or relatives, they must help you by observing the road and traffic situation to ensure safety throughout.

Before going out to practise you should first learn the Highway Code rules listed below:

Rules	38-41	Signs and signals.
Rules	43-51	Driving along.
Rule	69	Single-track roads.
Rules	95-96	Junction controls.

After learning the Highway Code rules, read the introduction and work through the lesson. Complete the checkpoint before going out in the car. Match your answers with those given at the foot of the page. Rub out any wrong ones and revise that particular part of the lesson.

Exercise 1 – How to control low speeds and move away quickly

To practise each step of this exercise, find a safe position on a slight uphill slope. Stop about a foot away from the kerb on a fairly wide road. Practise each step three or four times before moving on to the next.

Step 1 – Finding the holding point

With the engine running, select 1st gear, set the gas and find the holding point. Check that there are no other road users nearby and release the handbrake. Keep your feet still and hold the car stationary for two or three seconds.

If the car moves forwards, press the clutch down a little. If it rolls back, keep calm and raise the clutch slightly. ▼

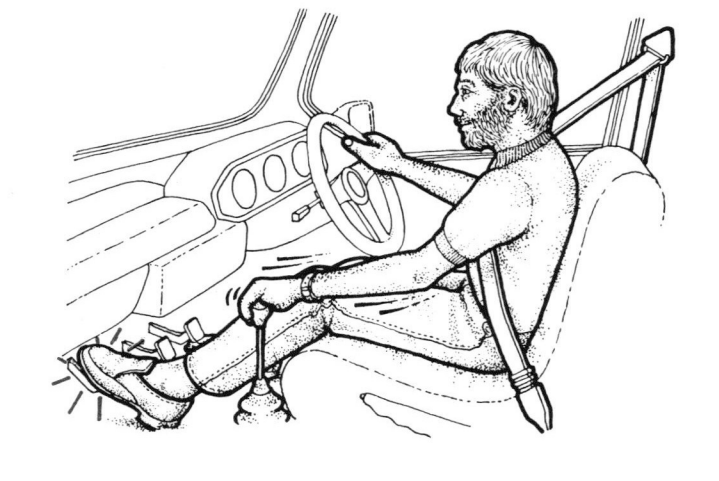

Step 2 – Moving off slowly with a slipping clutch

Follow the procedure in Step 1 and then raise the clutch slightly until the car creeps forwards.

Now press the clutch down slightly and try to creep forwards very slowly without stopping.
▼

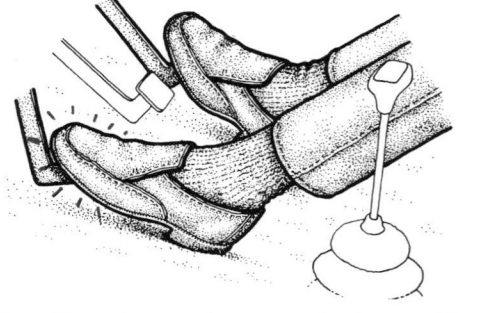

Step 3 – How to regain control when rolling backwards

Over-anxiety about rolling backwards is a major cause of loss of control on uphill junctions. This exercise should help to improve your confidence by showing how easy it is to regain control.

Follow the procedure in Step 1 and then push the clutch down slightly until the car starts to roll backwards. Let it roll two or three yards. To regain control, raise the clutch gradually until you can feel the car stopping.

If you let the pedal up too far or too quickly it may stall the engine or cause the car to jump forwards. At junctions this is more dangerous than rolling backwards a little.

Step 4 – How to move off quickly

Follow the procedure in Steps 1 and 2 until the car is creeping forwards.

To accelerate and move away quickly you should first start pressing the accelerator and then gently raise the clutch. Continue accelerating as you let the clutch up.

If the car jerks away, you need to press the accelerator a little harder or let the clutch up more slowly.

If the engine roars, let the clutch up a little more or use less pressure on the accelerator.

Remember to change into 2nd gear as soon as you have moved away.

Exercise 2 – How to control low speeds on downhill slopes

When moving off downhill there are times, such as in heavy traffic, at junctions or moving out from behind parked vehicles, when you will need to restrain your speed and move off very slowly. To do this you must keep the clutch down and use the footbrake to prevent the car rolling away too quickly.

Park on a quiet road facing downhill and practise moving off very slowly. Select 1st, or even 2nd gear for the exercise if you are on a very steep slope. Apply the footbrake to hold the car and then let the handbrake off.

Check that there are no other road users nearby and then gradually ease the footbrake up to allow the car to roll slowly forwards. Keep the clutch down when moving at very low speeds but remember to raise it when you have released the footbrake completely.

Stage

4

Exercise 3 – Learning to accelerate and change up through the gears

To practise this exercise find a fairly straight, wide and quiet road.

Move off and change into 2nd gear as soon as you can. Accelerate to about 15–20mph and then change to 3rd. Accelerate in 3rd to 25–30mph and then change to 4th.

After completing the exercise, find a safe position to stop. Discuss your performance with your instructor to find out where you can improve. Practise until you feel completely confident about when to change up to the next gear.

Exercise 4 – Learning to brake and change down through the gears

To practise this exercise you will need to be driving along at about 30mph in 4th gear. The instructor or supervisor should help by keeping a look-out and making sure it is safe for you to carry out each step of the exercise.

Step 1 – Changing down through the gears

When safe behind, use the brake gently to slow down to about 20mph. Release the brake and change to 3rd gear. Re-apply the brake gently and slow down to about 10mph. Release the brake and change into 2nd gear.

When safe, build your speed up through the gears until you reach about 30mph and practise again until you feel confident.

Step 2 – Changing from 4th to 2nd gear

When safe behind, use the brake gently to slow down to about 10mph. Release the brake and change from 4th gear into 2nd.

When safe, build your speed up through the gears until you reach about 30mph and practise again until you can do it smoothly and confidently.

Step 3 – Changing from 3rd to 1st gear

To practise this part of the exercise you will need to be driving along at about 20mph in 3rd gear.

When safe behind, use the brake gently to slow down until you have almost stopped. Push the clutch down, keep it down and release the brake so that the car keeps rolling forwards very slowly. Just before the car stops, change from 3rd to 1st.

When safe, move off again and accelerate, changing up through the gears until you reach about 20mph in 3rd and then practise again until you feel completely confident.

Exercise 5 – How to stop smoothly at a given point

To practise this exercise you must find a fairly straight, quiet road with plently of distinctive features such as telegraph poles, lamps or trees. The object is to stop with your front bumper level with these. You will need lots of practice to bring the car consistently to a smooth stop.

Drive along at about 25–30mph in 3rd or 4th gear. When safe behind, select a feature in the distance and cover the brake. This has a slight braking effect as the engine tries to slow down. Use this to help you judge how much braking pressure you will need. To begin with, squeeze the brake very gently. Gradually press it harder until you appear to be stopping just short of the required position.

Brake until you seem to be stopping short.

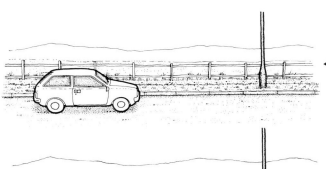

As you near the stopping point, push the clutch down and gradually ease some of the braking pressure. This lets the car roll up to the stopping point. Select 1st gear ready for moving away.

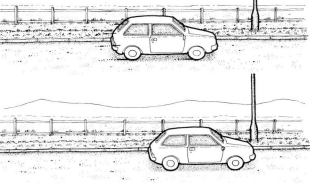

As the car comes to a rest with the front almost level with the stopping point, set the gas and find the holding point as described in Exercise 1, Step 1. Take care not to let the clutch up too far. Hold the car still for a second or two while checking it is safe to pull away.

Stage

4

Exercise 6 – How to stop in an emergency

Anticipation helps you to prevent emergencies. You will learn more about this and how to avoid accidents in Lesson 8.

For the moment you need to know that the sooner you spot any possible danger the earlier you can act ▶ on it. Taking precautions early, like slowing down, will reduce the likelihood of needing to brake hard.

Even experienced drivers sometimes find themselves having to stop quickly because they have failed to anticipate danger.

Make sure *you* can stop quickly before you go into heavy traffic.

To practise the emergency stop exercise you will need to find a quiet, fairly wide and straight road.

Your supervisor *must* demonstrate the stop signal before you move away and then ensure there are no other road users about before giving it.

In emergencies, there is little time to use the mirrors before braking so use them often as you drive along.

Step 1 – Braking firmly to a stop

On first attempts you should pull up with little more than the pressure needed for a normal stop.

When you receive the signal to stop, respond promptly and pivot quickly to the brake. Press the brake firmly but progressively and keep a firm hold of the wheel with both hands. Wait until the car has nearly stopped before pushing the clutch down. Pushing it down too soon increases the stopping distance and the risk of skidding. After coming to rest, put the handbrake on until it is safe to move off again.

Step 2 – Stopping quickly as in an emergency

Gradually increase the braking pressure until you can stop the car quickly and without skidding or swerving. Be realistic about the distance it will take to stop. In wet conditions it takes much longer. Use a lighter pressure on the brake or you may lock the wheels and skid.

Exercise 7 - Steering practice and checking the instruments

Step 1 – Anticipating when to turn the wheel

Find a quiet road with plenty of sharp bends.

Approaching left bends move your left hand towards the top of the wheel ready to pull it down and steer round the bend or corner.

Approaching right bends move your right towards the top of the wheel ready to pull it down and steer round the bend or corner.

Step 2 – Steering with one hand

Although you must keep both hands on the wheel as much as possible, there are times when you need to switch the lights, wipers and other controls on or off.

Find a straight, quiet road where you can steer with one hand while you use these controls and practise winding the windows up and down.

Step 3 – Giving arm signals

Practise giving arm signals for left and right turns and for slowing down.

Step 4 – When to check the instruments

The instruments help to keep you informed about how the car is running. Ignoring warning lights can result in breakdowns or serious damage.

You should stop and get help if malfunctions occur with the braking system, if you have an overheated engine or low oil pressure. Look well ahead and only glance quickly at one instrument at a time. Only do this when there is nothing much happening on the road and you can spare the time. Find out from your car handbook what these symbols mean.

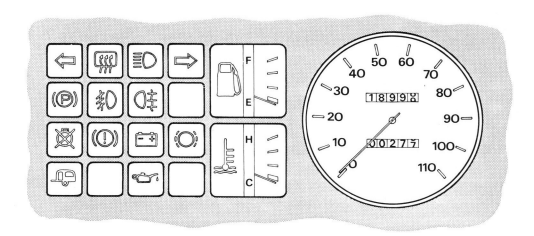

LEARN TO DRIVE

4 Stage

Checkpoint

1. At 30 mph your thinking distance is:
   [a] 30 feet.
   [b] 45 feet.
   [c] 75 feet.

2. At 30 mph your braking distance is:
   [a] 30 feet.
   [b] 45 feet.
   [c] 75 feet.

3. At 30 mph your overall stopping distance is:
   [a] 30 feet.
   [b] 45 feet.
   [c] 75 feet.

4. At 40 mph your overall stopping distance is:
   [a] 75 feet.
   [b] 120 feet.
   [c] 240 feet.

5. At 70 mph your overall stopping distance is:
   [a] 175 feet.
   [b] 245 feet.
   [c] 315 feet.

6. Signs giving orders are mostly:
   [a] rectangular.
   [b] triangular.
   [c] circular.

7. On wet icy roads the gap between you and the vehicle ahead should be:
   [a] at least doubled.
   [b] quadrupled.

8. A green traffic light means:
   [a] go.
   [b] you may proceed if the way is clear.

9. The traffic light sequence is:
   [a] red – amber – green – amber.
   [b] red – red & amber – green – amber.

10. Stop light signals mean:
    [a] I am going to stop.
    [b] I am slowing or stopping.

11. A solid line across the end of a road means:
    [a] stop at the stop sign.
    [b] give way at the traffic signal.

12. Double broken lines across the end of a road mean:
    [a] stop at the stop sign.
    [b] give way to traffic in the major road.

13. Double solid lines along the road mean:
    [a] do not overtake.
    [b] do not cross or straddle the line.

14. A long white line with short spacings along the centre of the road:
    [a] provides advance warning of a hazard.
    [b] means you must not cross the line.

15. To stop in the shortest distance, should you:
    [a] brake as hard as you can and push the clutch down at the same time?
    [b] brake until the wheels lock?
    [c] brake firmly and press the clutch down just before you stop?

16. During an emergency stop, should you:
    [a] keep two hands on the wheel?
    [b] press the brake and clutch together?
    [c] brake hard and change down?

17. Not checking instruments may result in:
    [a] breakdowns.
    [b] damage.
    [c] both [a] and [b].

Checkpoint answers

1. [a] 2. [b] 3. [c] 4. [b] 5. [c]
6. [c] 7. [a] 8. [b] 9. [b] 10. [b]
11. [b] 12. [b] 13. [b] 14. [a] 15. [c]
16. [a] 17. [c]

Driving with Confidence

Introduction

To practise this lesson you will need to find a quiet estate with wide roads, rounded corners and not too many parked cars.

First you should practise the mirror-signal-manoeuvre routine turning left and right into side roads.

Once you have mastered these you can practise the system approaching the end of a road. At first you should practise on junctions which provide you with a clear view into the main road.

Once you can cope with quiet estates you can practise on sharper corners and major roads with more traffic. However, you should still avoid the very busy junctions and those on uphill gradients.

Only when you have completely mastered the system and junction routines and you feel confident in yourself, should you practise on busier roads, at junctions on hills and those where your view is restricted.

Before going out to practise you should first learn the following Highway Code rules:

Rules	70-73	Markings along the road.
Rule	91	Passing parked vehicles.
Rules	93-96	Approaching junctions.
Rule	98	Mini roundabouts, controls and signs.
Rules	100-105	Junction controls and turning right.
Rules	108-109	Turning left.
Rule	65	Pedestrians when turning.
Rule	94	Left signals and emerging.
Rule	110	Roundabout procedure.
Rule	114	Signals at roundabouts.

After learning the rules and reading the introduction, work through the lesson and complete the checkpoint before going out in the car. Match your answers with those given at the foot of the page. Revise anything you feel doubtful about.

More about the mirror-signal-manoeuvre routine

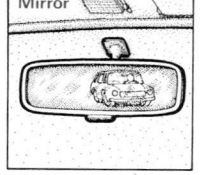
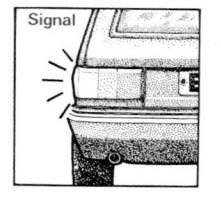

The rule is to slow down before changing down. If you need to change gear, do it as you finish braking or after you have released the footbrake.

Approaching too fast will result in frequent and unnecessary stops. Your approach speed should be such that it allows you time to look properly. This will involve a lower speed than that needed simply to stop.

Get into the habit of using this system well before approaching a junction or an obstruction in the road. Look in the mirror and try to judge the speed and position of vehicles behind you. Assess the distances involved and how others may be affected by your movements. Decide whether your manoeuvre is safe and if a signal will help to warn or inform other road users about your intentions. Allow time for them to see and respond to your signal.

Remember that a manoeuvre is any action involving a change in your speed or position.

Positioning your car correctly helps to confirm your signals and intentions. The proper position provides you with the maximum view and safety margins. Others can see you, you can see them and your view of any possible dangers is improved.

Try to get your car into position well before you reach a turn or other hazard. This will cause the least inconvenience to the flow of traffic.

Approach junctions and other hazards slowly enough to look for a safe opportunity to proceed. To do this, you will need to slow down before reaching the junction and leave time to select a lower gear ready to accelerate away.

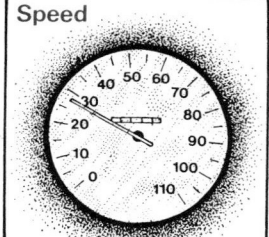

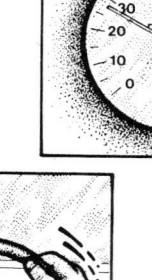
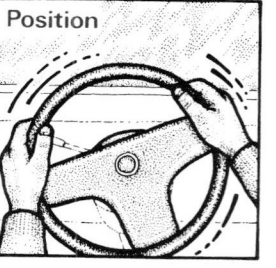

Start looking early as you approach the junction. Make sure that you can see properly before deciding to go forward.

Excessive approach speeds are often the cause of late, unnecessary stops and unsafe decisions to proceed before the driver can see that the way ahead is clear.

Using the MSM routine at junctions

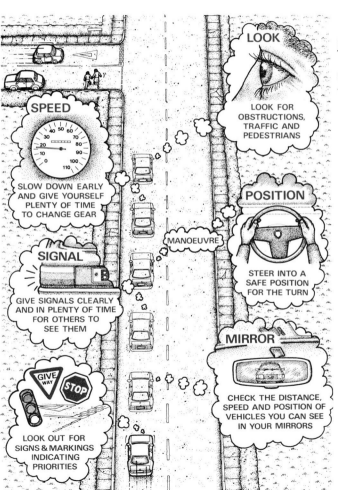

Where to position the car when turning and for normal driving

For normal driving and turning left position the car about two to three feet from the kerb.

Before turning right you should position the car just to the left of the centre of the road.

After completing a turn you should return to the normal driving position of about two to three feet from the left edge.

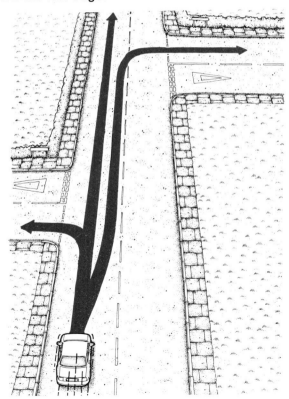

The point of turn when going right

One of the main dangers when turning right is from oncoming traffic. You must normally let approaching vehicles go first. Slow down and hold back until they have passed the junction. If you reach the point of turn first, stop and wait just short of it.

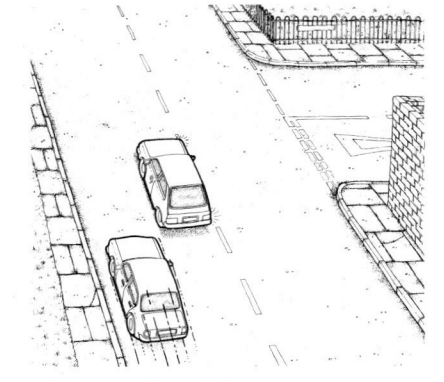

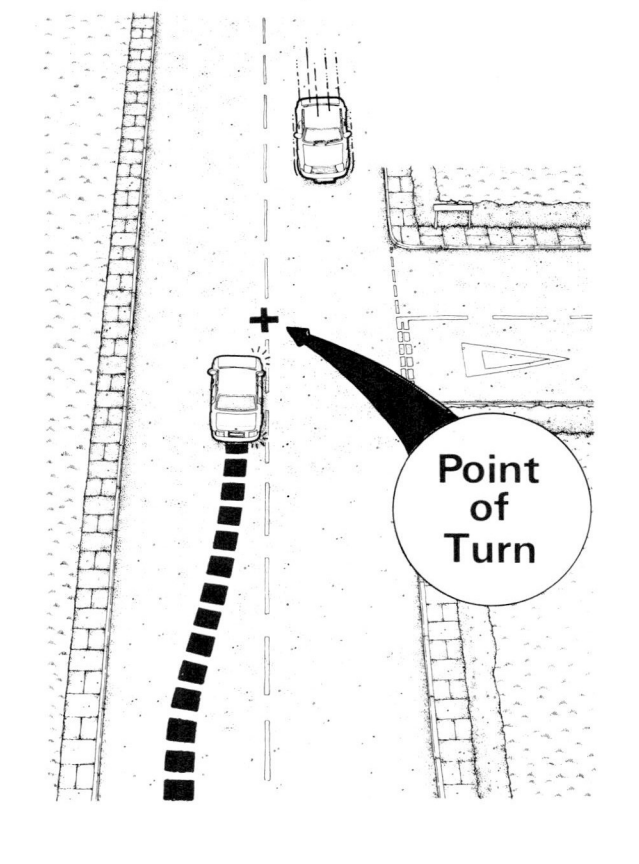

Position before turning right

Get into a position early and maintain it. On a wide road this normally allows following vehicles to pass on your nearside. Look into the side road for obstructions and give way to pedestrians crossing the entrance to the turning. Wait in this position until your way is clear.

Dangers to avoid when turning left

When turning left it is important for you to maintain a constant position two to three feet out from the kerb.

If drivers get too close to the kerb when turning, the rear wheel may cut in and cause them to strike it. This could damage the tyre leading to its failure or to its becoming illegal to use.

Positioning the car too close to the kerb sometimes results in drivers swinging too wide and into the path of cars approaching the end of the side road from the opposite direction.

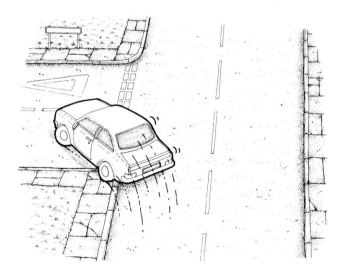

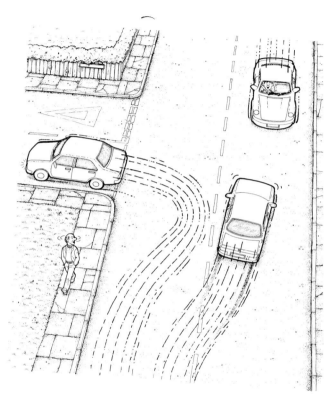

When travelling too close to the kerb some drivers swing out just before turning. As they slow down, following drivers sometimes pull out to pass. Both practices are potentially dangerous.

Stage 5

Dangers to avoid when turning right

Remember when turning right that the correct position for your car is just to the left of the centre of the road. Maintain this position up to the point of turn and avoid wandering back in.

Meet oncoming traffic safely when turning right. Watch out for vehicles approaching in the middle of the road. Keep well to the left until you can safely move into the correct position for turning.

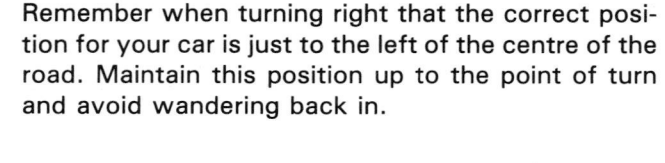

How to avoid cutting right-hand corners

Move up to the point of turn slowly and make sure that you can see into the new road before turning. Avoid cutting the corner and watch out for vehicles approaching the end of the side road.

When turning right at the end of a narrow road, position the car well to the left to leave room for traffic turning into the side road.

When you are approaching the end of a side road yourself, watch out for drivers who do cut corners and be prepared to hold back for them.

Watch out for limited views of oncoming traffic when turning right

Cross oncoming traffic safely when turning right. Sometimes your view may be restricted near bends and hill crests. There may be an approaching vehicle just out of sight.

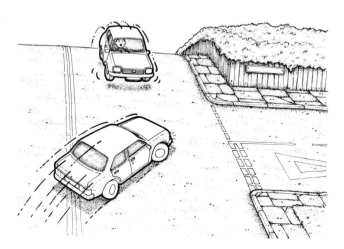

Give way to pedestrians crossing the road you are turning into

Give way to pedestrians crossing any road into which you are turning. Watch out particularly for those with their back to you. They may not have seen you and could walk into the road without look-ing. In some instances, where they are walking towards the road, it may be appropriate to sound the horn lightly.

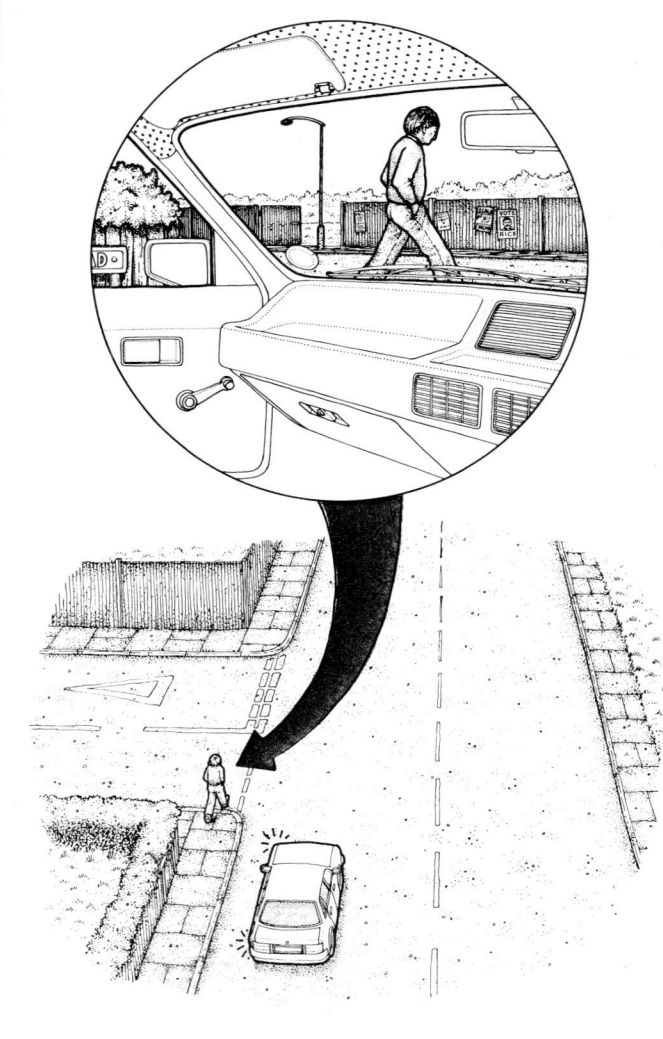

How to approach the end of a road

Approaching T-junctions

Approach the end of a road slowly and keep a look-out for pedestrians.

Give yourself time to look into the main road. There are usually hedges or buildings restricting your view of traffic. If you stop too soon you will not be able to see properly.

Keep a special look-out for cyclists or motorbikes travelling along close to the kerb.

Stage

5

Give way to pedestrians crossing as you approach the end of a road

When approaching a junction, look out for pedestrians and give way to any who may be crossing the end of the road. Be particularly careful when approaching busy shopping streets.

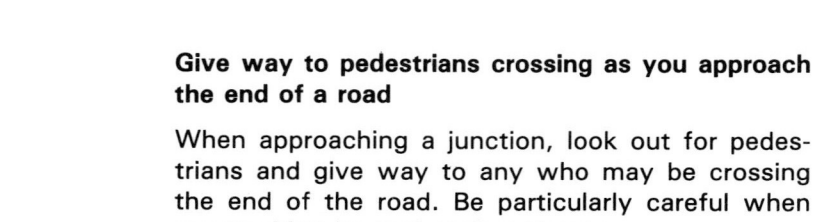

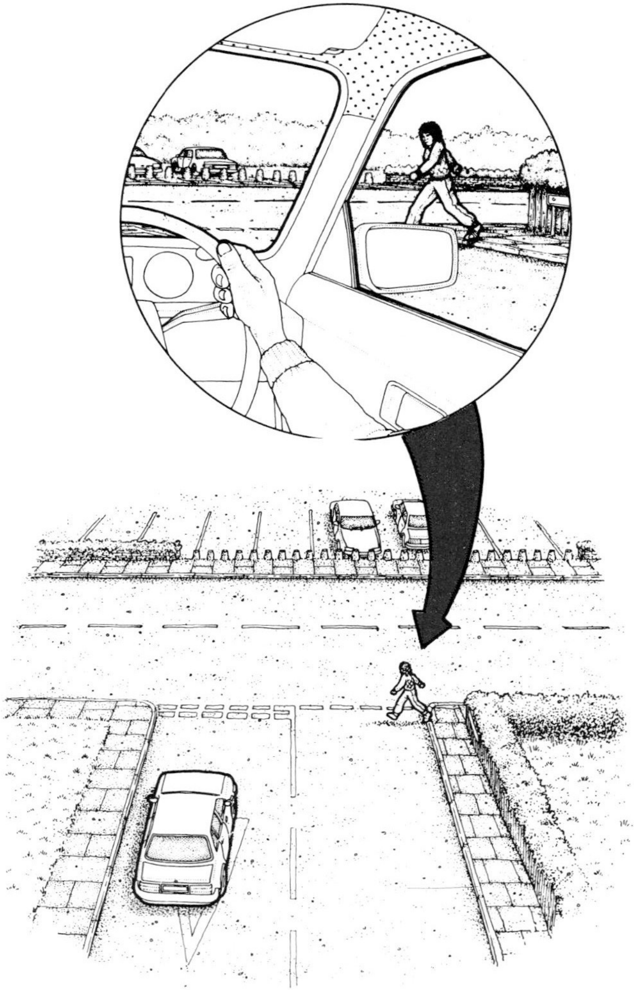

Look both ways before moving into a major road

Vehicles parked near junctions will seriously restrict your view of traffic travelling along the main road.

Creep slowly forwards looking both ways. Look particularly for approaching vehicles hidden behind the obstruction. Make sure you can see properly before deciding to proceed.

Watch for vehicles approaching from the left along your side of the road.

How to approach an uncontrolled crossroad

When driving along quiet side streets you will sometimes see crossroads with no signs or markings.

Unrestricted sightlines sometimes make them difficult to spot. Be on the lookout for them.

Approach slowly and be prepared to give way to traffic moving along the other road. The other driver may not have seen the danger.

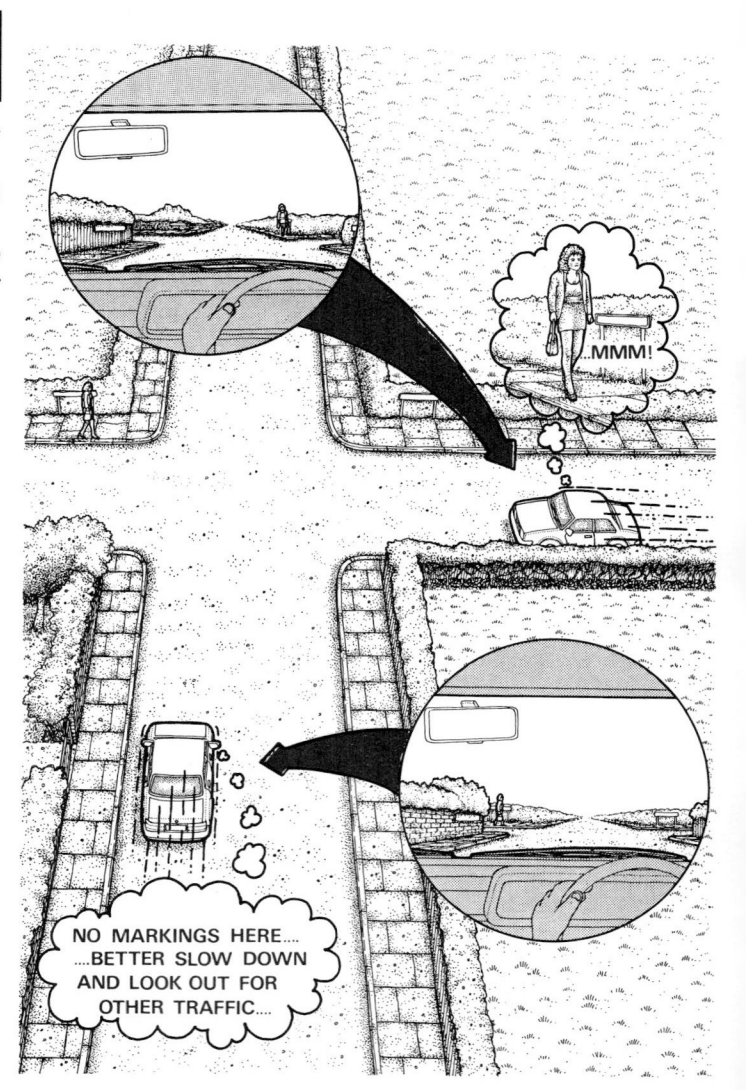

When to give way to oncoming vehicles

When vehicles are parked on your side of the road, move towards the centre without impeding oncoming vehicles. This overtaking position gives you a better view and reduces the risk of getting boxed in. Be ready to slow down early and hold well back to give way to oncoming traffic.

You should normally be prepared to wait in the hold-back position until you can leave four or five feet clearance.

Sometimes, in traffic hold-ups, it may be necessary to pass through much narrower spaces between other vehicles at very low creeping speeds.

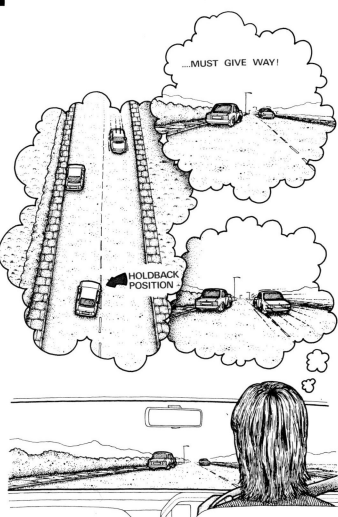

....MUST GIVE WAY!

HOLDBACK POSITION

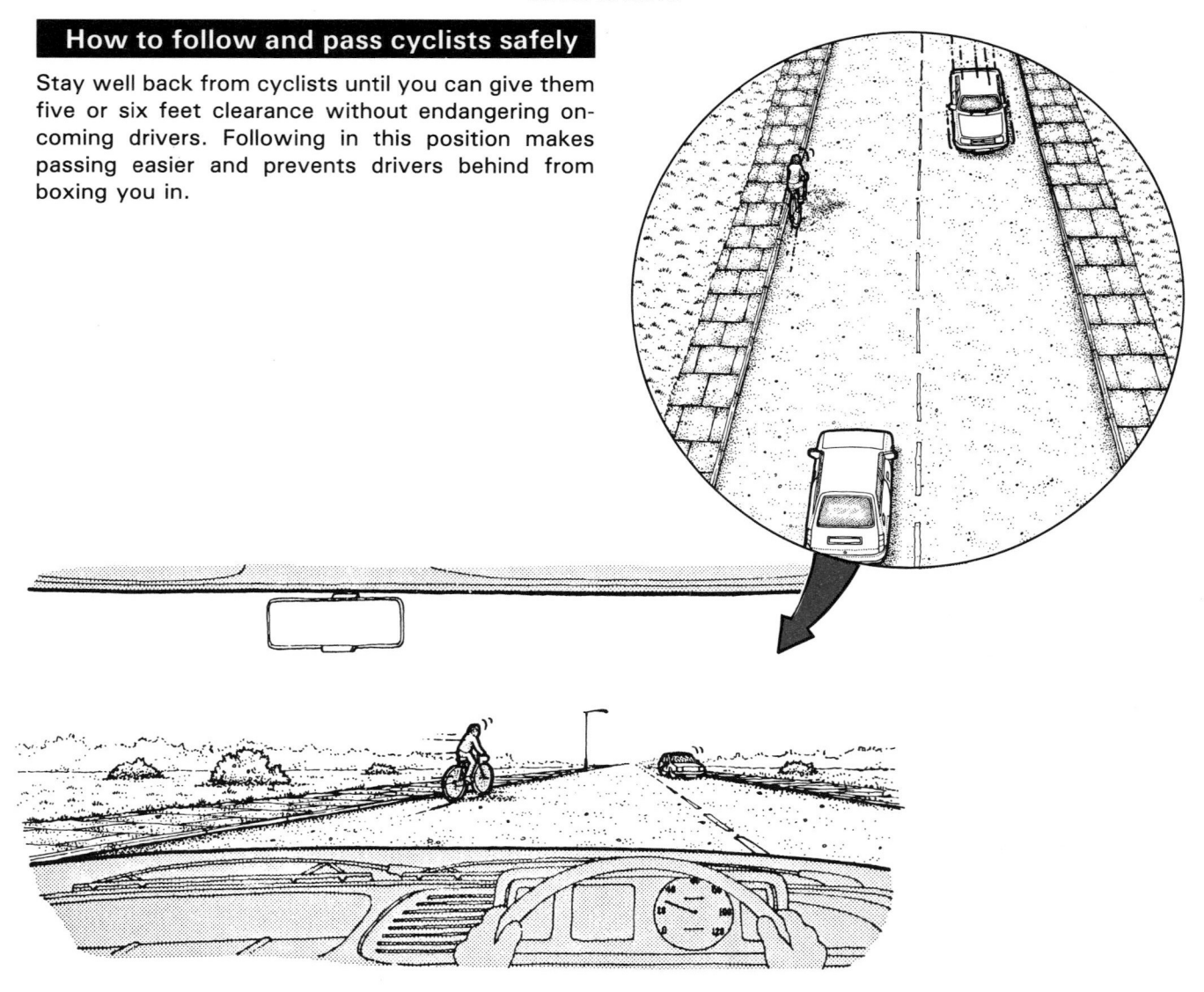

How to follow and pass cyclists safely

Stay well back from cyclists until you can give them five or six feet clearance without endangering oncoming drivers. Following in this position makes passing easier and prevents drivers behind from boxing you in.

Stage

5

Checkpoint

1. The position for turning left is:

   [a] as close to the kerb as possible.
   [b] about two to three feet from the kerb.

2. The position for normal driving is:

   [a] as close to the kerb as possible.
   [b] in the centre of your side of the road.
   [c] about two to three feet from the kerb.

3. The correct sequence is:

   [a] mirror-signal-manoeuvre.
   [b] mirror-signal-speed.
   [c] mirror-signal-look.

4. Turning left at a roundabout should you:

   [a] signal only when you reach it?
   [b] signal on the approach?

5. Turning right at a roundabout should you:

   [a] signal right on the approach?
   [b] signal left as you pass the exit before the one you want?
   [c] both [a] and [b]?

6. Approaching a left bend, should you position:

   [a] two to three feet from the kerb?
   [b] towards the centre line?

7. A safe following distance from another car is:

   [a] one yard for each mph of your road speed.
   [b] two seconds back.
   [c] both [a] and [b].

8. If a driver behind is too close, should you:

   [a] stay further back from the car in front?
   [b] flash your brake lights?
   [c] drive faster?

9. When waiting for an opportunity to pass a cyclist, should you normally:

   [a] keep close to the kerb.
   [b] stay well back but towards the centre of the road.

10. The correct sequence is:

    [a] speed-position-look.
    [b] look-speed-position.
    [c] position-speed-look.

11. The point of turn is:

    [a] where the centre of the road you are turning from crosses the centre of the one you are turning into.
    [b] where the give way line changes to an edge marking.

12. Approaching parked vehicles, would you:

    [a] look for people walking out from behind them?
    [b] slow down if your view is restricted?
    [c] both [a] and [b]?

13. A manoeuvre is any action involving a:

    [a] change in speed.
    [b] change in direction.
    [c] both [a] and [b].

14. The correct sequence is:

    [a] mirror-signal-look-position.
    [b] mirror-signal-speed-position.
    [c] mirror-signal-position-speed.

15. The main danger when turning right into a side road is:

    [a] left turning traffic.
    [b] oncoming traffic.

16. Clearance for parked cars should normally be:

    [a] up to two feet.
    [b] four to five feet.
    [c] at least seven feet.

17. If a car is parked on your side should you normally:

    [a] take right of way over oncoming traffic?
    [b] give way to oncoming traffic?

18. The position for turning right at the end of a narrow road is normally:

    [a] just to the left of the centre.
    [b] well to the left.

Checkpoint answers

1. [b]   **2.** [c]   **3.** [a]   **4.** [b]   **5.** [c]   **6.** [a]

7. [c]   **8.** [a]   **9.** [b]   **10.** [c]   **11.** [a]   **12.** [c]

13. [c]   **14.** [c]   **15.** [b]   **16.** [b]   **17.** [b]   **18.** [b]

Stage

5

How to Reverse

This lesson consists of a series of structured exercises which you can start practising from the end of Lesson 4. Practise them as soon as you are able to control the car at very low speeds. Introduce the exercises progressively with the other things you are learning in Lessons 4, 5 and 7. You should master all the exercises before you start Lesson 8.

During your first few attempts at these exercises, a professional instructor will help by keeping a lookout for other road users. This will help to develop your control and confidence quickly and safely. If you are learning with friends or relatives, they must also help you initially by looking out for those nearby.

As soon as you can, however, you must take complete responsibility for your own observations and decisions.

Before going out to practise you should first learn the Highway Code Rules 116 to 118 inclusive. Work through the lesson and complete the checkpoint before going out to practise.

Exercise 1 - Revising low speed control

Revise Steps 1 and 2 of Exercise 1 in Lesson 4 and practise again for a few minutes on a quiet road. You will find this on page 40. At first you should practise the exercise while driving forwards. A good test to see if you have really mastered the art of controlling the car at low speeds is to practise moving out from behind a parked vehicle.

Exercise 2 - How to move out from behind a parked vehicle

Find a vehicle parked on a wide, level road and pull up between 8 and 10 feet behind it. To move off you will need to control the clutch and go much more slowly than usual. Make extra observations to the front and rear before you move off and look round again as you are pulling out. Use a slipping clutch as practised in Exercise 1 to keep the car moving very slowly as you pull out. Turn the wheel boldly until you are clear of the parked vehicle and then turn it back.

When you have mastered the exercise on a level road practise up and down slopes.

Exercise 3 – How to reverse slowly in a straight line

Practise on a quiet road. Turn round in your seat until you can see the road clearly through the back window. You should be able to see the kerb on both sides. Go slowly and watch out to the front and rear for approaching traffic. Keep a special look-out for pedestrians before you start moving backwards.

I MUST LOOK WELL BACK DOWN THE ROAD AND CONCENTRATE ON STEERING STRAIGHT....OR.....

BEING AWARE OF THE KERB ON BOTH SIDES OF THE ROAD HELPS ME TO JUDGE WHEN MY CAR IS GOING STRAIGHT...... AND PREVENTS....

...IT'S MORE IMPORTANT TO STEER STRAIGHT THAN TO FINISH CLOSE IN TO THE SIDE.....QUICK GLANCES AT THE KERB ARE ALL I'LL NEED TO JUDGE MY DISTANCE FROM IT.......

Exercise 4 – How to drive into a parking space between two vehicles

You will need a space at least two and a half times the length of your car. Almost stop just before the space keeping about three feet from the parked vehicles. Drive on slowly and steer in until your front wheel nears the kerb; then steer right to bring your wheel into line. Centre your car in the space.

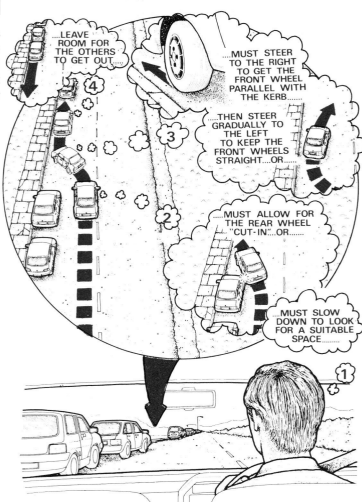

...LEAVE ROOM FOR THE OTHERS TO GET OUT.....

...MUST STEER TO THE RIGHT TO GET THE FRONT WHEEL PARALLEL WITH THE KERB.......

...THEN STEER GRADUALLY TO THE LEFT TO KEEP THE FRONT WHEELS STRAIGHT....OR.....

...MUST ALLOW FOR THE REAR WHEEL "CUT-IN"....OR......

...MUST SLOW DOWN TO LOOK FOR A SUITABLE SPACE........

Stage 6

Exercise 5 – How to turn the car round in the road

At first practise on a fairly wide road. Once you have moved over the centre of the road be ready to brake gently if your car starts rolling down the camber.

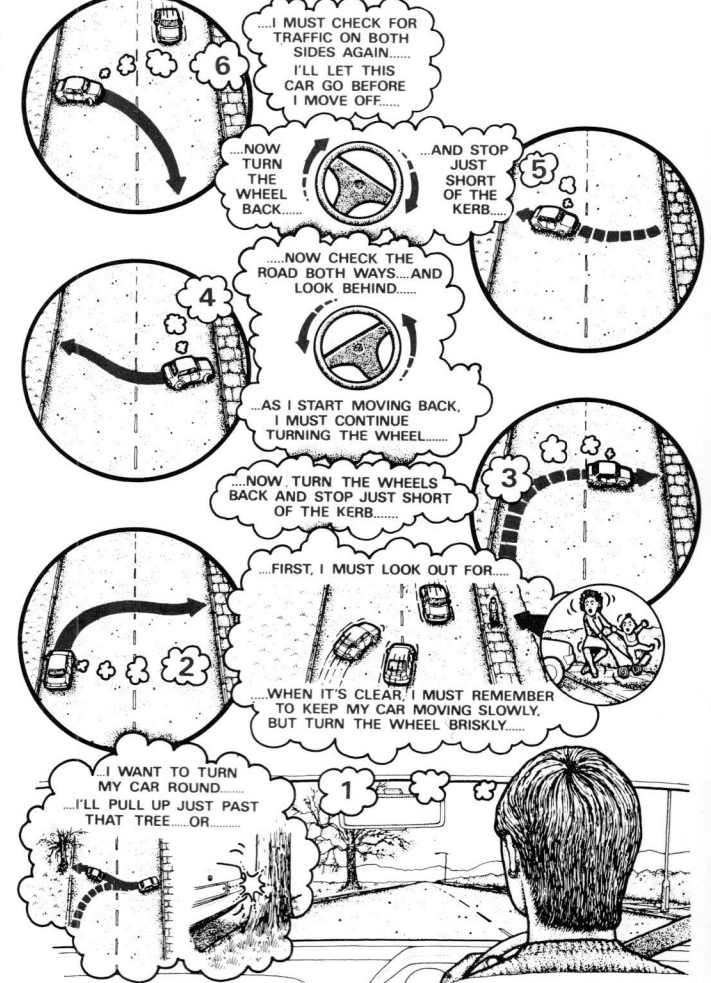

Exercise 6 – How to reverse into a road on the right

Do this if there is no opening on the left or if you are driving a vehicle without side windows. Wait at the 'point of turn' for oncoming traffic and then pull over to the right side, drive just past the corner and stop a little way out from the kerb.

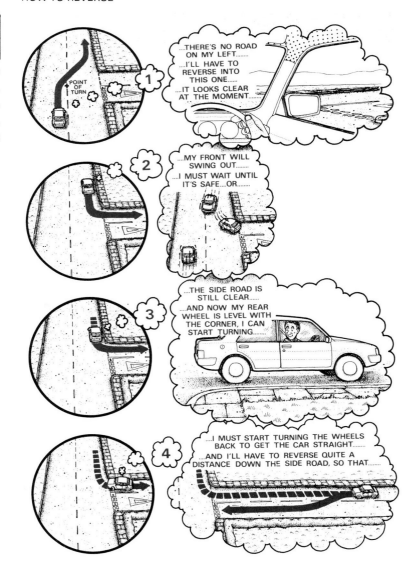

Stage 6

Exercise 7 – How to reverse into a road on the left

Drive just past the corner and stop a little way out from the kerb. Watch out for people nearby while you drive back two to three car lengths into the side road. Be prepared to pull forwards out of the way of vehicles approaching the end of the side road from your rear.

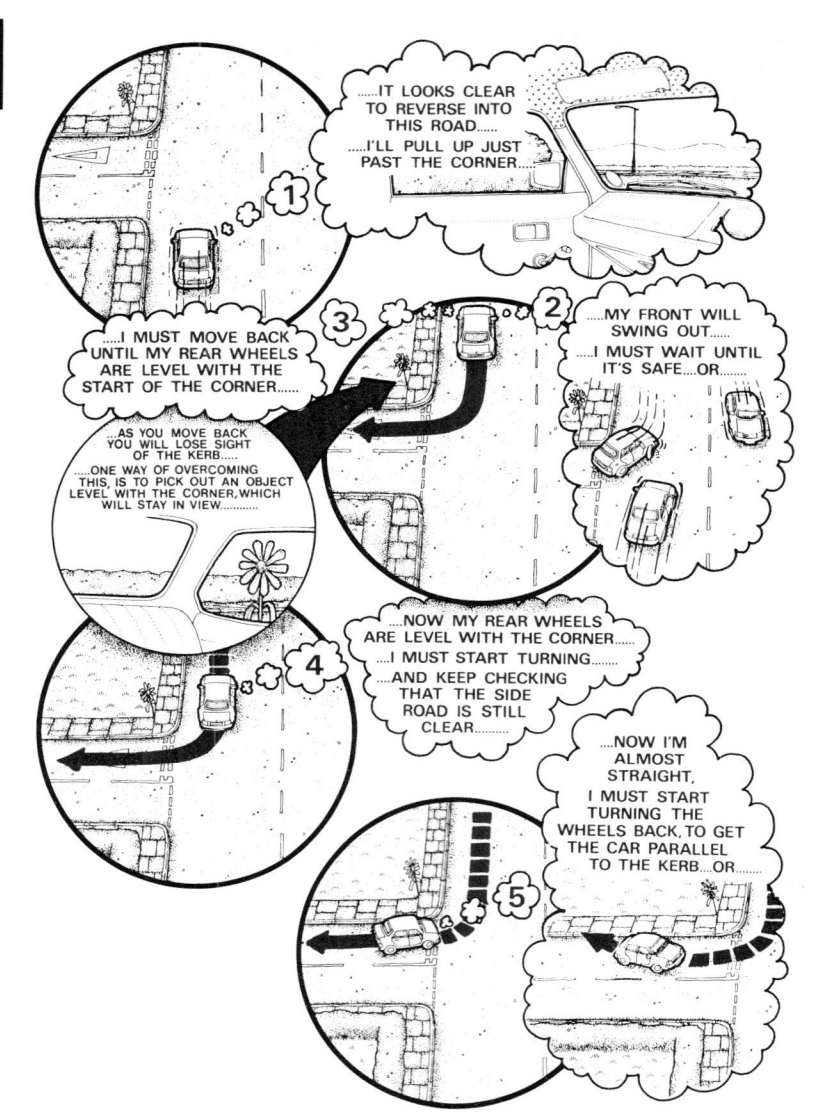

Exercise 8 - How to reverse into a parking space

Find a space at least one and a half times the length of your car. Pull up about three feet away from and just forwards of the leading vehicle. If this is likely to cause a serious disruption to the traffic flow you should look for somewhere else to park.

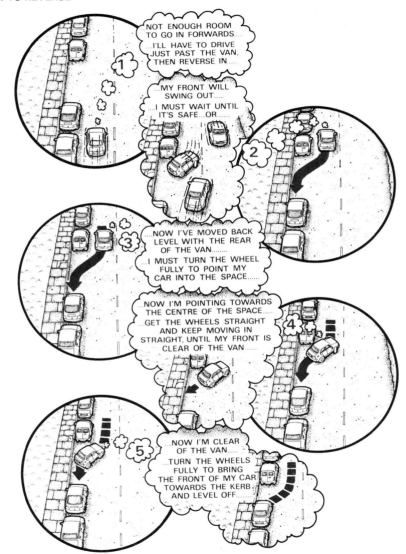

Stage 6

Stage 6

Checkpoint

1. Before reversing should you normally:

   [a] sound the horn?
   [b] make sure the road is clear?

2. If you are unable to see when reversing should you:

   [a] sound the horn?
   [b] get someone to help?

3. To turn your car round you should:

   [a] reverse into a side road.
   [b] drive into a side road and reverse out.
   [c] either [a] or [b].

4. You should not normally reverse:

   [a] more than 15 yards.
   [b] more than is necessary.

5. When turning in the road you must:

   [a] complete the manoeuvre in three movements.
   [b] keep full control of the vehicle?

6. When preparing to reverse into a space between parked vehicles should you position:

   [a] close to the leading vehicle?
   [b] just past the leading vehicle?
   [c] well past the leading vehicle?

7. Before opening your door you should:

   [a] check there is no one about.
   [b] ensure no danger will be caused.

8. When manoeuvring should you:

   [a] drive slowly?
   [b] turn the steering wheel slowly?

9. Before reversing should you first:

   [a] turn round in your seat?
   [b] select reverse gear?

10. When parking between two vehicles should you:

    [a] centre your vehicle in the space?
    [b] leave your car close to the one in front?
    [c] leave your car close to the one behind?

11. When reversing should you normally:

    [a] take right of way?
    [b] give way to others?

12. Vehicles parked near junctions:

    [a] make it difficult for drivers to see.
    [b] make it difficult for pedestrians to see.
    [c] both [a] and [b].

13. Before leaving your vehicle you must:

    [a] ensure the handbrake is on.
    [b] ensure the engine and headlamps are off.
    [c] both [a] and [b].

Checkpoint answers

1. [b] **2.** [b] **3.** [a] **4.** [b] **5.** [b] **6.** [b]

7. [b] **8.** [a] **9.** [a] **10.** [a] **11.** [b] **12.** [c]

13. [c]

Common Sense and Experience

Introduction

When you have mastered the car control skills in Lesson 4 and the basic rules and routine procedures outlined in Lesson 5 you should start thinking about gaining some experience on busier roads and in traffic.

You may feel a little anxious about this at first, but try to keep calm and take things one step at a time. The only way to build up your confidence in these conditions is to practise in them. At first, you should practise in busier conditions on the outskirts of a city or large town. Gradually work your way nearer to the town centre over three or four sessions.

Try to get plenty of experience on a wide variety of roads and junctions. Practise driving in laned traffic and on one-way streets, turning on to and off dual carriageways, dealing with roundabouts and turning right at busy traffic-light controlled crossroads.

Before going out to practise you should first learn the Highway Code rules listed below. Work through the lesson and complete the checkpoint before going out on the road.

Rules	119-123	Use of lights, flashing headlamps and horn.
Rule	126	Hazard warning flasher.
Rules	52-53	Priority vehicles and buses.
Rules	56-68	Pedestrians and animals.
Rules	74-83	Driving in lanes.
Rule	109	Turning across bus lanes.
Rules	111-113	Roundabouts with multiple lanes.
Rule	115	Roundabout procedure – other vehicles.
Rule	97	Crossing dual carriageways.
Rule	107	Turning right from a dual carriageway.
Rule	99	Box junctions.
Rule	102	Green filter signals.
Rule	106	Junction procedure – opposed right turn.
Rule	54	Microphones and telephones.

How to avoid accidents with other vehicles in front and behind

Follow other vehicles at a safe distance and stay even further back from large and slow moving ones. This improves your view of the road and traffic ahead and helps you to anticipate the actions of the driver in front. You also get more time to respond.

Where other drivers are following you too closely, drop even further back from the vehicle ahead of you. This gives you more breathing space and extra time to brake gently; it also gives those behind you more time to pull up if you do brake.

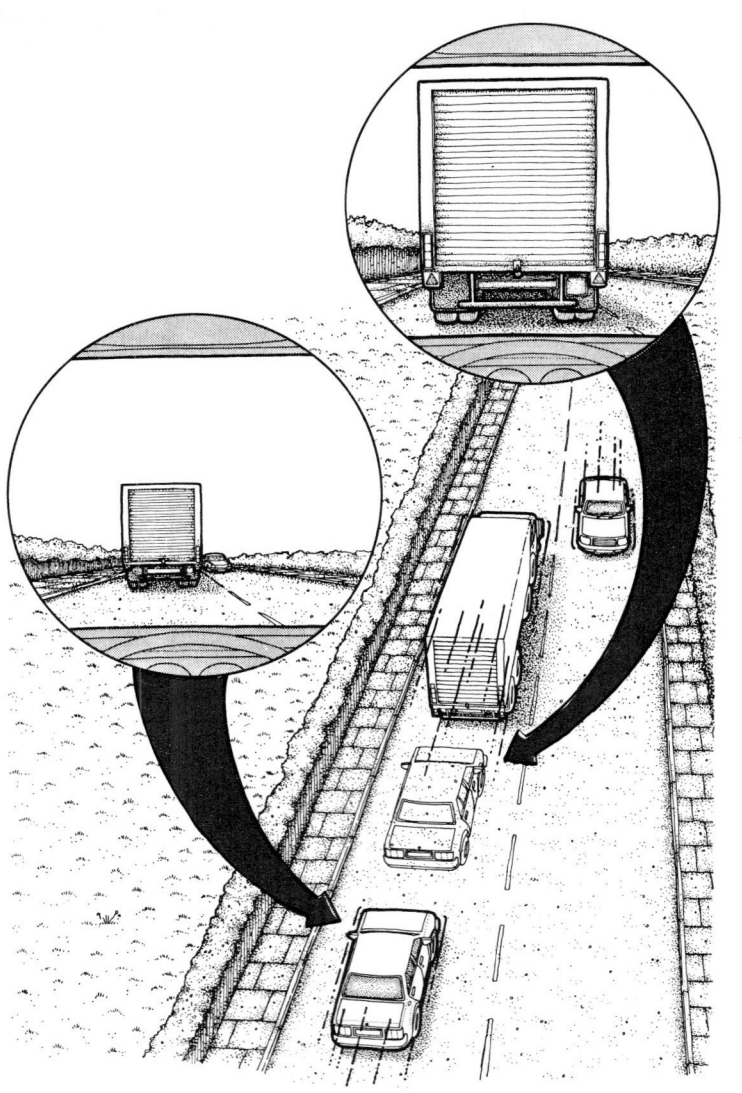

How to act on signals given by other road users

Watch out for signals given by the drivers of vehicles in front of you and anticipate their actions. When a signal is flashing, the driver is almost sure to slow down before a manoeuvre. Anticipate this and carry out the mirror-signal-manoeuvre routine yourself.

If the vehicle ahead is turning right, position your car well to the left and decide whether or not there is room to pass on the nearside. Be prepared to slow down and wait. If the space is too small to get through safely, hold back. Remember the other driver may have to wait for oncoming traffic.

If the driver in front is signalling left, the vehicle may be either stopping or turning. Move into an over-taking position but hold well back as drivers waiting in the side road may emerge.

Even when you are sure the driver in front is turning, you should expect him to stop and wait if the side road is blocked or if there are any pedestrians crossing.

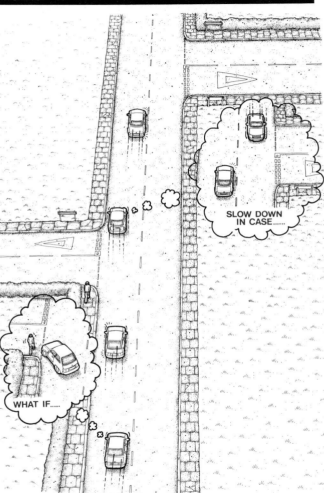

Stage

7

How to make fuller use of the mirrors

Simply looking in the mirrors is not sufficient. You must also act sensibly on what you see in them. Watch the traffic behind and take note of, and stay alert to, the presence of vehicles moving into the blind spots at your sides.

Let others overtake if they wish and leave room for them to return safely to the lane ahead of you. Remember to use the side mirrors before changing lanes and leaving roundabouts.

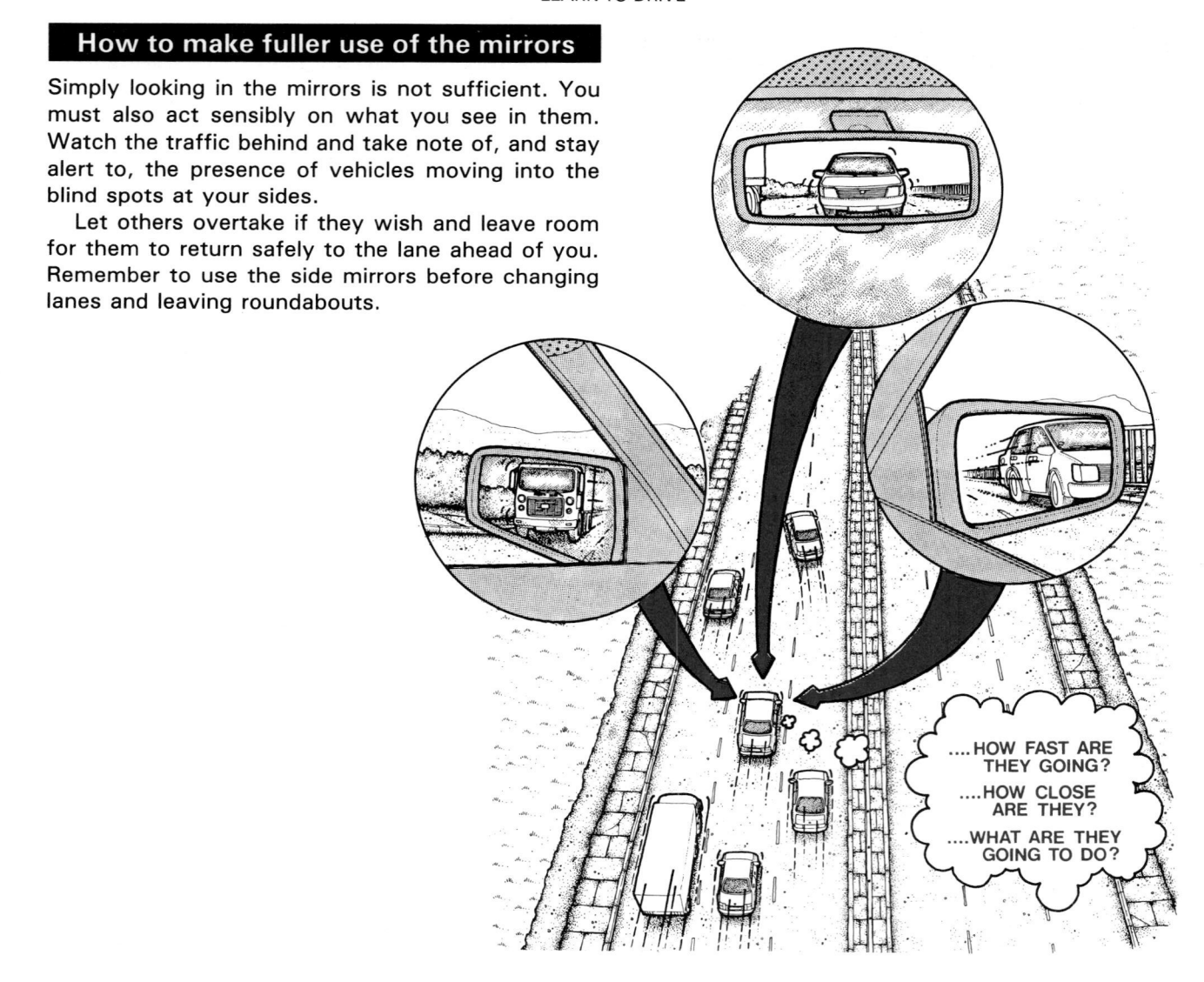

Anticipating a need to use the mirrors

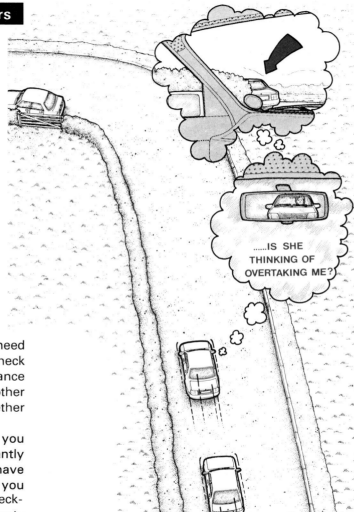

......IS SHE
THINKING OF
OVERTAKING ME?

Approaching a bend, consider the action you may need to take if there is a car parked just out of sight. Check your mirror beforehand so that you know in advance what is happening behind you. Assess how close other vehicles are, how fast they are travelling and whether they are likely to overtake you.

When the parked car comes into view, you already have the information to decide instantly whether a signal is necessary. You should also have worked out whether it is safe to pull out or if you must hold back to let an overtaking driver pass. Checking the mirror again before pulling out should merely confirm what you already know.

Deciding whether to signal

Use your mirrors often and after giving a signal always check to see how others are responding to it.

If you are not sure whether a signal is really necessary, it is usually advisable to give one. Giving a signal, however, will not make an unsafe action safe.

Signals are required more frequently for pulling out to pass obstructions when following traffic is approaching quickly or is already in a lane to your right, or when you are driving in fog or poor light.

Signalling too often for passing parked cars can reduce its impact and lull following drivers into ignoring those signals given later for turning right. Unless following too closely, drivers behind can normally see ahead of you. They can usually tell from your speed and position that you intend to pass parked vehicles. If you pull out late, however, you will need to signal more frequently.

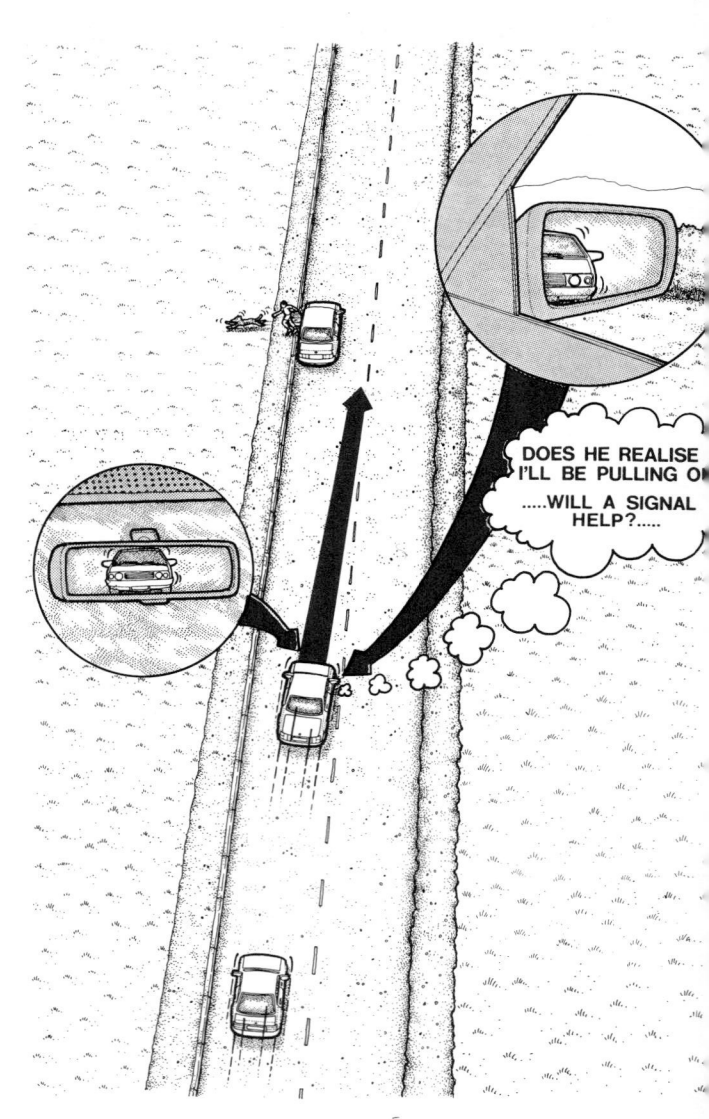

Deciding when to signal

Signals should normally be given early so that others have time to respond. Some signals, however, need to be delayed; for example, if you want to turn left and have yet to pull out to pass a parked vehicle.

When turning left wait until you are up to the first road before signalling to take a second. Drivers in the first road may pull out if they think you are turning in. However, try to give as much warning as possible to vehicles behind you.

Signals given at the wrong time may panic others into taking unnecessary evasive action. Before giving any signal you should consider its effect on others. For example, delay the right turn signal for changing lanes when drivers behind are overtaking.

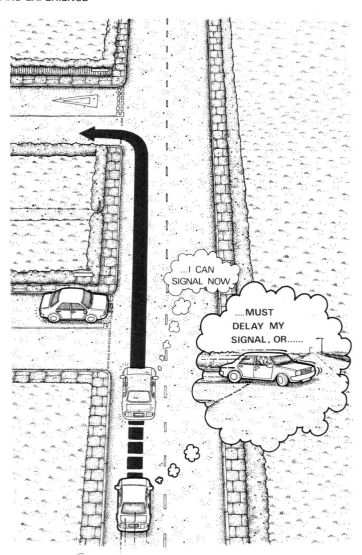

How to cope with driving in lanes

When driving along dual carriageways and other multi-laned roads you should drive in the middle of your lane. You should normally keep to the left lane unless turning right or overtaking. However, look and plan well ahead to make sure that you do not get boxed in behind any parked vehicles. If you see others wanting to move out into the lane ahead of you, hold back and let them. Avoid straddling the lanes when approaching junctions and passing stationary cars or other obstructions.

On one-way streets take the most convenient lane for driving straight ahead and expect other vehicles to pass you on either side. Pedestrians sometimes get confused about which direction to look for traffic. Watch out for them stepping into the road, especially if you are in the right-hand lane.

Driving on dual carriageways

When driving along dual carriageways you must use the mirrors more frequently. Look out for obstructions blocking your lane, vehicles ahead slowing down and those moving through the central reserve.

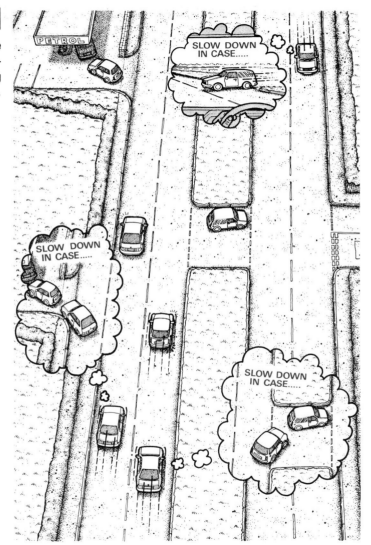

Turning right on to a dual carriageway

When turning right on to a dual carriageway, decide if the opening in the central reserve is wide enough to offer your car protection from traffic moving along the road.

NO! TREAT BOTH CARRIAGEWAYS AS ONE ROAD

YES! TREAT EACH CARRIAGEWAY AS A SEPARATE ROAD

WILL THERE BE ENOUGH ROOM TO WAIT IN THE MIDDLE?

Dual carriageway ahead

How to change lanes safely in a queue of slow moving traffic

If you find yourself in the wrong lane, and unable to change safely, be prepared to stay in it and miss your turning.

When you are in queues of very slow moving or stationary traffic and you need to change lanes try eye contact. Put your signal on and then look at the driver just to your rear. Try to make eye contact and smile, he is almost certain to let you in. Drive slowly and change your direction positively but very gradually. Avoid sudden changes in direction or spurts of speed and watch out for motorcyclists approaching from behind who may be travelling at high speed between the traffic lanes.

How to benefit from using eye contact

The next time you are waiting to move off into a main road containing a queue of slow moving or stationary traffic, look at the drivers and try to establish eye contact. If you can attract their attention in this manner and smile, they are almost certain to hold back and let you out.

How to approach traffic-lights and anticipate them changing

Be prepared to start slowing down early when approaching red traffic-lights. This will give them more time to change. If you have to wait, you should normally apply the handbrake and select neutral.

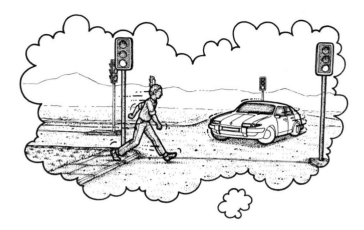

The green light means you may proceed providing it is safe to do so. If your intended exit is blocked, wait at the stop line until you can move through the junction without blocking it for others. Before proceeding, you should look for vehicles moving along the other road and for oncoming drivers who might turn right across your path. This is important and helps you decide whether it is safe to proceed. Watch out for pedestrians crossing the road and be prepared to hold back for them.

When approaching a green light remember that all the other colours mean stop. Try to anticipate the possibility of the light changing and be ready to pull up. At some point on the approach, however, you will find yourself too close to stop safely. Once you have passed this point you should normally continue.

Working things out as you approach will speed your reactions. Check how close following vehicles are and how fast they are travelling. Continually reassess what you will do if the lights change. This saves critical split seconds if the amber light appears by enabling you to make an instant decision to go on or pull up.

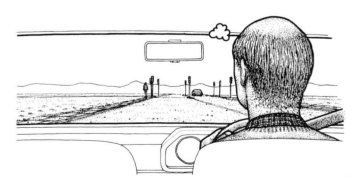

Where to position when turning or going straight ahead at crossroads

To drive straight ahead or turn left at a busy junction you should normally approach and stay in the left lane. Keep to this lane unless you can see reasons for not doing so.

At junctions with two or more lanes marked with arrows pointing straight on, think ahead and choose the most convenient one. To do this look ahead for obstructions and use your knowledge of the area.

To turn right from a busy multi-laned road, you should normally approach in the right-hand lane. One of your major priorities is to get into position early and without disrupting other traffic. To do this, try to maintain your speed while you check your mirrors for traffic approaching from behind and to your sides. Reducing speed before you get into position may encourage following traffic to overtake and prevent you from carrying out your manoeuvre. Be prepared to increase your speed so that you can move safely over or if necessary hold back and wait for a larger space in the traffic. Think ahead and try not to get boxed in.

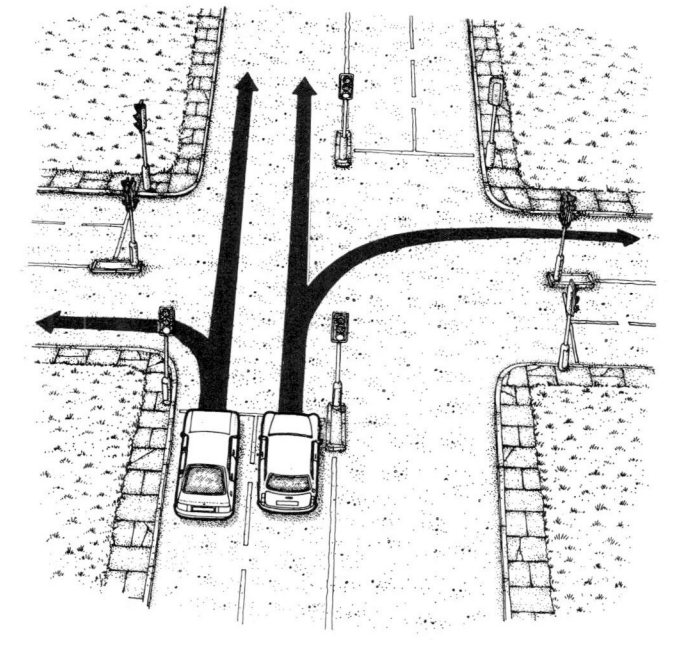

Choosing the most appropriate lane for going straight ahead

Look and plan well ahead to help you select the most appropriate lane for going straight ahead at busy junctions.

Use the right-hand lane if there are parked vehicles or any other obstructions blocking the left lane at the far side of the junction.

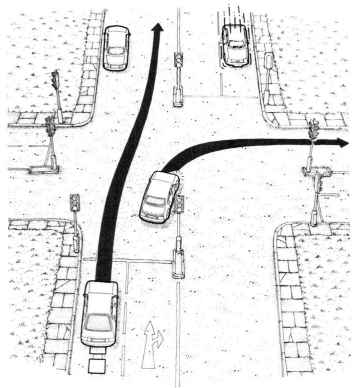

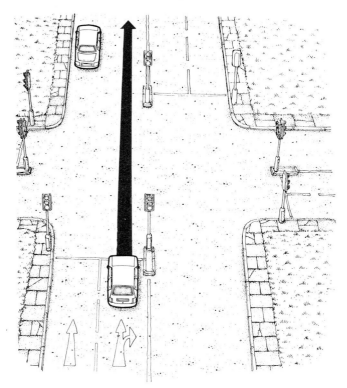

Watch out, however, for right turning vehicles. These are sometimes delayed for long periods while they wait for oncoming traffic. If you have to wait behind them you may be held up for a long time.

Where there is right turning traffic it is normally better to choose the left lane, even where there are obstructions at the other side of the junction.

Be prepared to give way to and wait for oncoming traffic

When turning right at traffic-lights, remember that oncoming vehicles usually have a green light at the same time. Watch out particularly for oncoming traffic which is likely to travel straight on through the junction or turn left. You must give way to such vehicles.

Wait just short of the point of turn for a suitable break in the traffic. If it is very busy, you may have to wait for the lights to change before you get an opportunity to turn. When this happens you should normally clear the junction as quickly as you can but be sure that the oncoming traffic is stopping before you proceed.

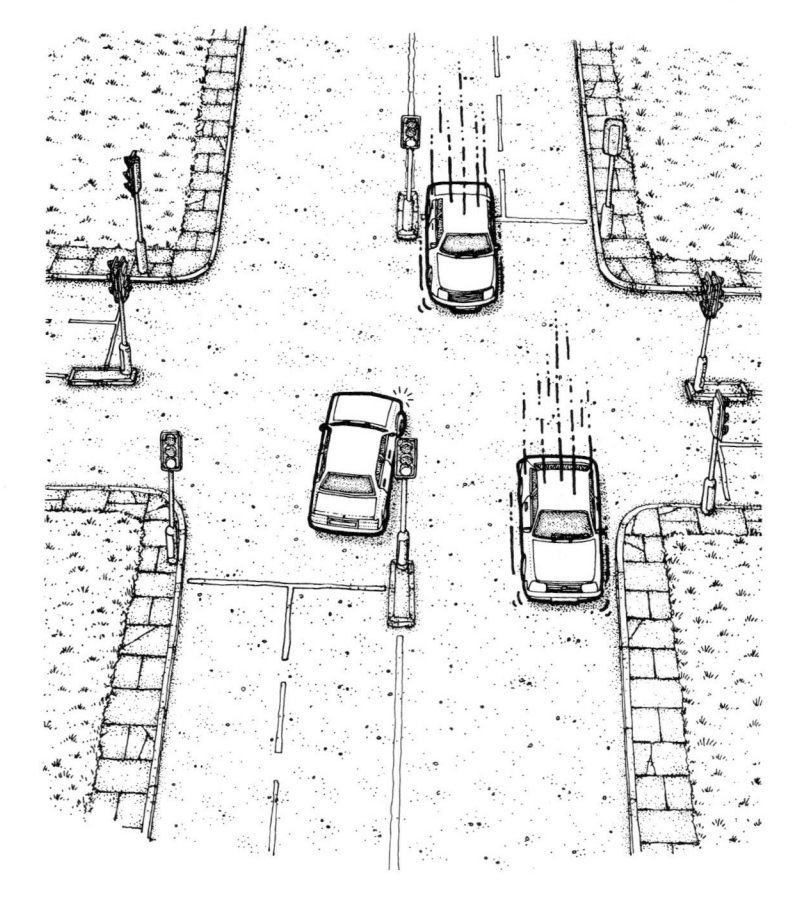

What to do at traffic-light filter arrows

Where you see a left filter arrow, the nearside lane is sometimes marked for left turning traffic only. Avoid using this lane unless you are turning in that direction.

When the arrow is lit you may turn left regardless of any other lights which may be showing. Proceed cautiously and look for other traffic moving in from your offside.

Where you see a right filter arrow, you may turn right regardless of any other lights showing. Check that the oncoming traffic is slowing down and stopping before you turn.

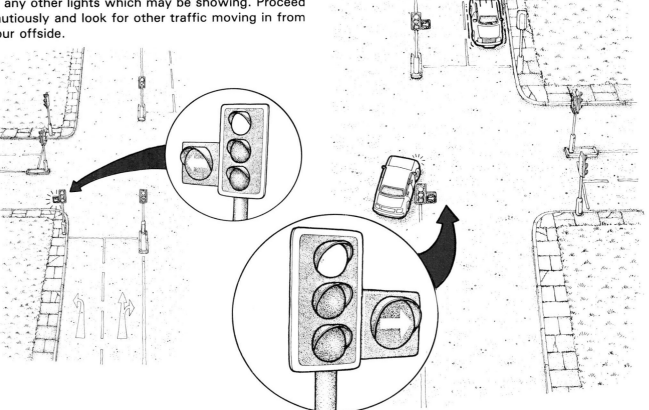

How to make an offside to offside turn

Where more than two vehicles are involved the road will become blocked unless those second in line hold back. Move slowly forwards to the point of turn and turn around the rear of the other vehicle. Look, and be prepared to wait, for any oncoming vehicles which are travelling through the junction in the far lane. Other oncoming vehicles waiting their turn in the queue will severely restrict your view of any approaching vehicles.

How to make a nearside to nearside turn

This method is sometimes appropriate because of the size or position of other vehicles or the junction layout and markings. It enables more vehicles to turn in less time and gives an improved view of the new road. Move slowly forwards watching the position of the oncoming vehicles. Steer gradually to the right looking for traffic travelling through the junction. Look and be prepared to wait for oncoming traffic.

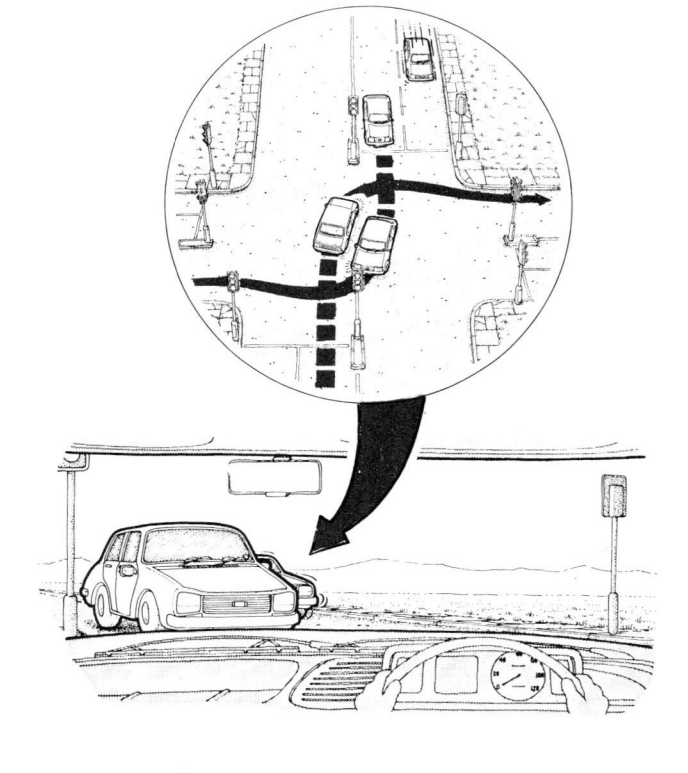

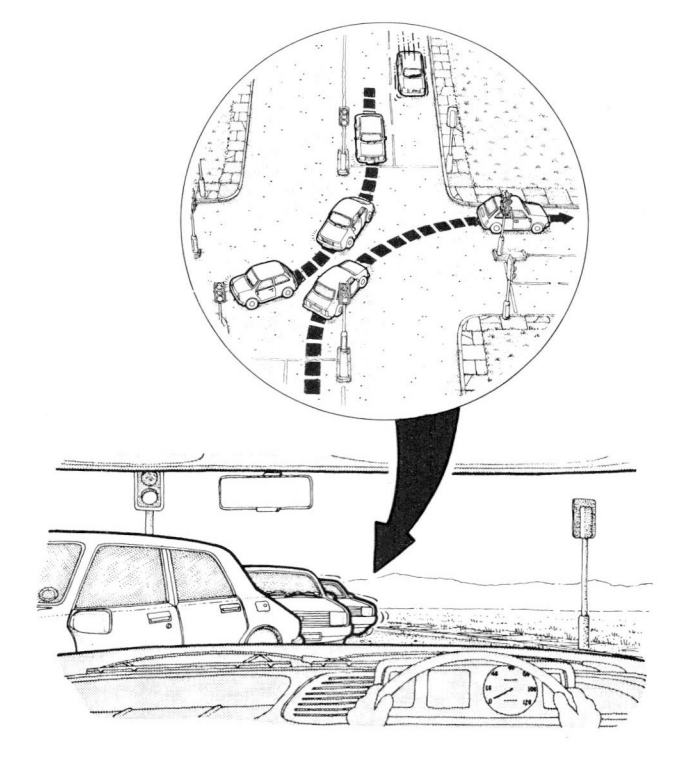

How to choose the most appropriate lane for turning left or right

Look out for junctions where road markings vary from normal and get into position as soon as you can. At junctions with two or more lanes marked for the direction you wish to take, choose the most convenient one. To do this you need to know where you are going at the next junction and which lane you will need when you get there. Look, think ahead and use your know-ledge of the area. At first, however, you may have to rely on your instructor's knowledge.

After selecting a lane, drive in the middle of it and stay there throughout the turn. Unless you need the right lane at the next junction you normally return to the left lane on completing the turn. Before doing this check there is no one turning at your side.

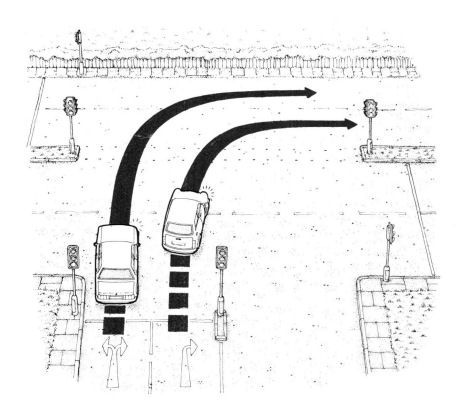

Stage

7

How to approach roundabouts and select a position

Long before you reach a roundabout, look for, and make a mental note of, the position of your exit road. Take short, frequent looks as you approach and try to time your arrival to coincide with a gap in the traffic. Let traffic coming from your right go first.

When turning left, signal and approach in the left lane. Keep the signal on and maintain the left lane into the exit road.

If you wish to follow the road ahead, you should normally approach in the left lane and stay in it round the roundabout. As you pass the first exit give a left signal to indicate you are leaving by the next exit.

When turning right, signal and approach in the right-hand lane. Keep the signal on and maintain the right lane into, and round, the roundabout. Approaching the second exit check for vehicles in the nearside lane and ensure it is safe to cross it. Change the signal to left and leave by the next exit. You should normally leave in the left lane if it is clear.

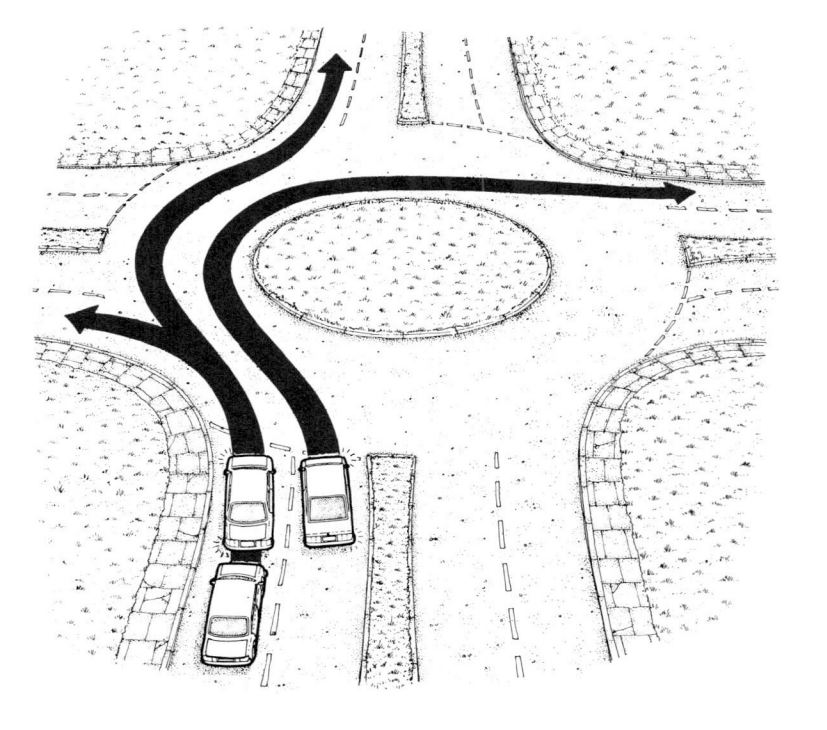

What to check when leaving a roundabout

Build up and maintain a reasonable speed on the roundabout. Failing to do this, especially when you are in the right-hand lane, may result in other drivers passing on your nearside. Always check for vehicles on your left before leaving the roundabout. Where vehicles are coming through on your nearside, or the left-hand lane is blocked, leave in the right-hand lane.

Choosing the most appropriate lane when approaching roundabouts

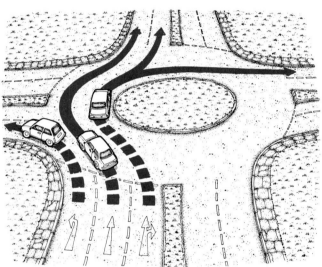

Look well ahead for road markings giving directions which vary from the basic rules. Get into position early and stay in the middle of your lane.

Stage 7

How to plan ahead to the next turn and choose an appropriate lane

Avoid last-minute changes in position over short distances by working out your course in advance. To do this you need to know where you are going at the next junction and which lane you will need there. Look ahead and use your knowledge of the area. At first, however, you may have to rely heavily on your instructor.

When negotiating a number of junctions within 100 yards or so of each other, choose a lane which puts you in the correct position for the next junction.

For example, the lane you need to approach the second of these two roundabouts influences your position at the first. After selecting the correct lane you will be able to stay in it throughout a series of turns.

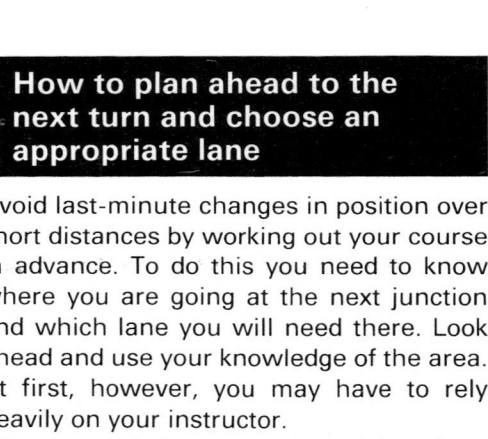

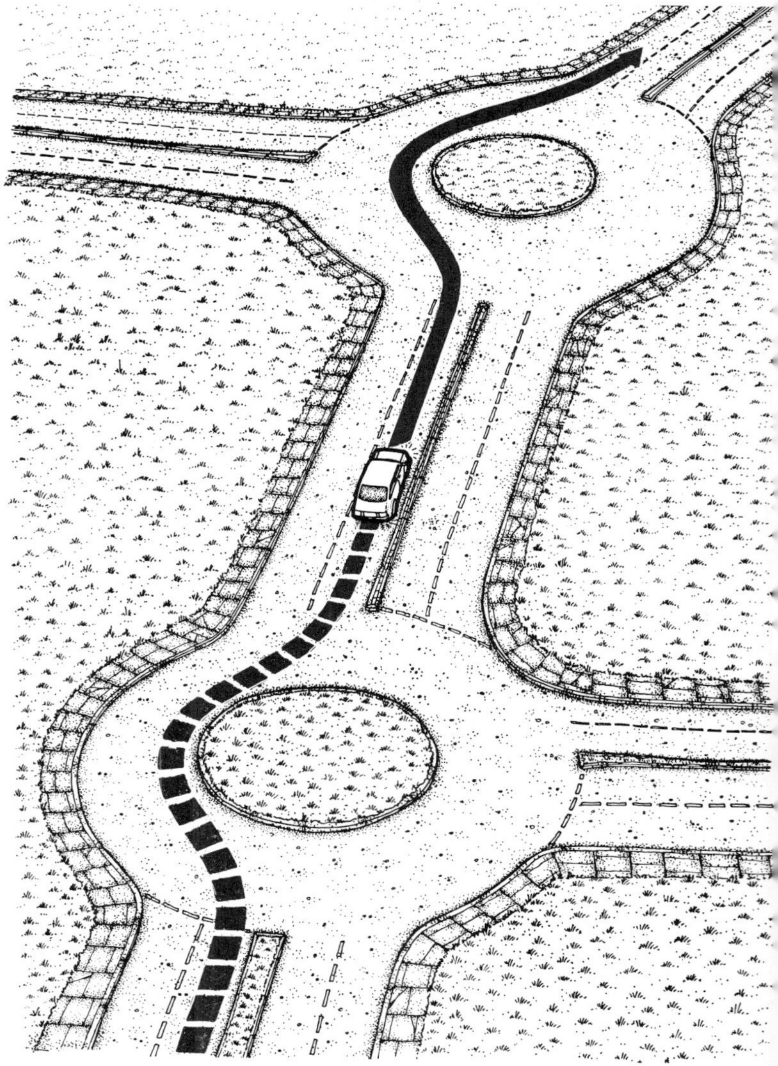

What to look out for when approaching a pedestrian crossing

Watch out for, and give precedence to, pedestrians on zebra crossings. Look out for people standing near or moving towards crossings. Work out in advance whether they are likely to cross and be ready to slow down. You must be able to pull up if they step out.

If your view of the pavement to either side of the crossing is blocked by parked vehicles or any other obstruction, slow down as if people were crossing. Be ready to stop until you can see it is safe to continue.

Remember to park well away from any kind of pedestrian crossing.

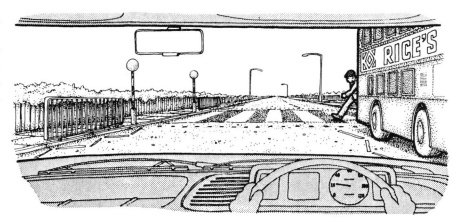

Stage
7

Approaching a zebra crossing

You must not overtake on the approach to pedestrian crossings. When driving in laned traffic you may pull level with the leading vehicle in another lane which is also waiting at the crossing, but you must not proceed in front of it.

Treat a zebra crossing with a refuge in the middle as two separate crossings but watch out for pedestrians on the other side nearing the central reserve as they may walk straight across.

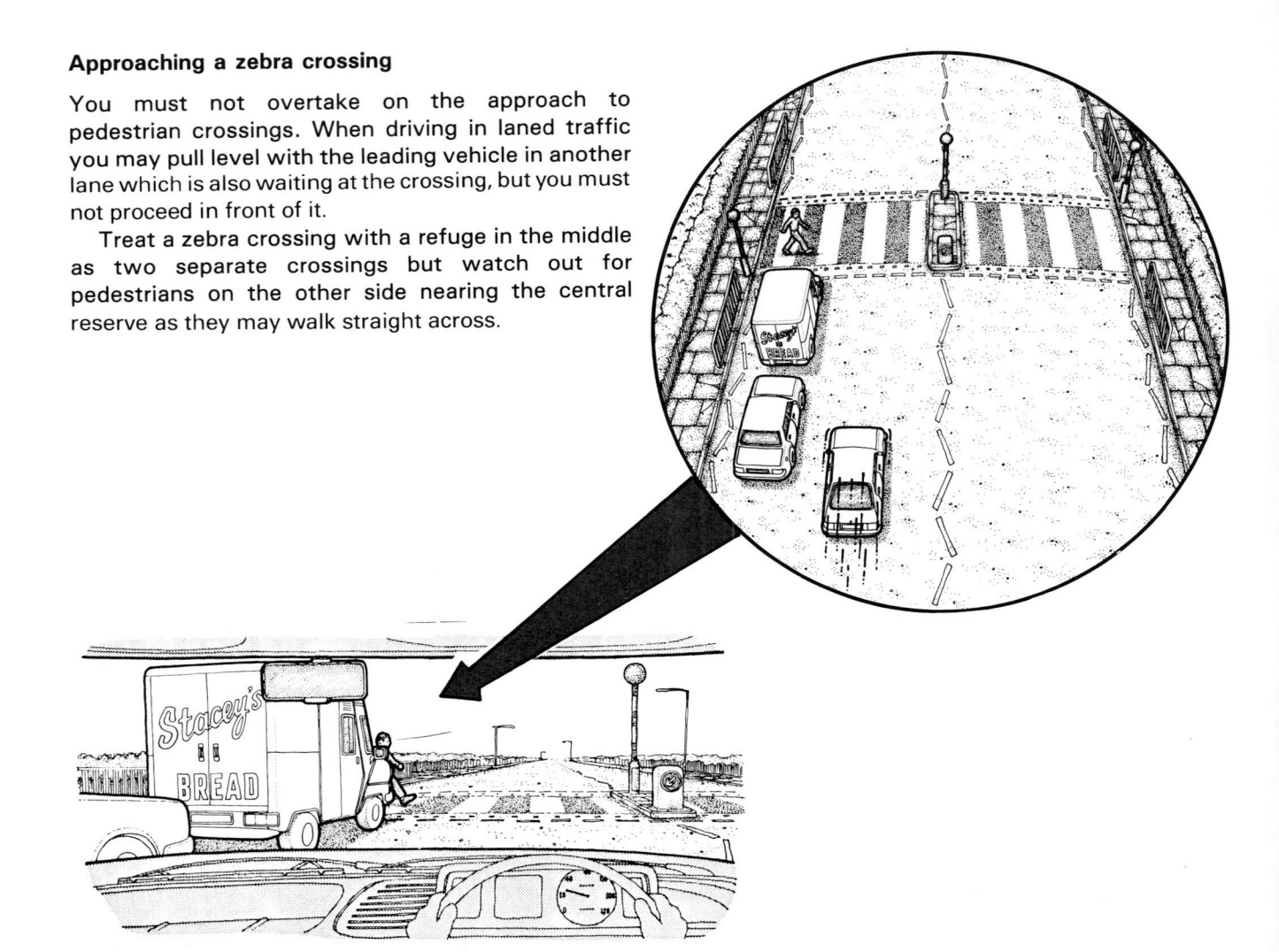

What to do when approaching a crossing

Where you see pedestrians waiting to cross, slow down early. If you hold back soon enough they usually cross before you reach the crossing. Look at them and try to make eye contact. This helps ▶ reassure them that they have been seen. If you have time, give an arm signal for slowing down. This lets the pedestrians know what you are doing and also warns other drivers.

It is important to avoid giving any other kind of invitation to people to cross. Other drivers may not be stopping.

Some pedestrians find it more difficult to cross the road than others. For example, you should allow extra time for the old or infirm to cross. Be patient with them and go slowly. People with prams find it difficult to put their foot on to the crossing without first pushing the pram out. Others with small children also need more time. Young people are often impulsive and may dash out on to the crossing.

After giving precedence to a pedestrian you do not need to wait until they are completely across, but do not startle them by driving too close or too fast. They may change their mind about crossing.

At pelican crossings give precedence to people who have already started to cross when the amber light begins to flash. Once they have crossed you may proceed.

Watch out for people making a last minute dash on to the crossing after the lights have started flashing. Be prepared to let them go, but do not invite others who are waiting to cross to start to do so.

Watch out for traffic-light controlled crossings at junctions

The timing of the sequence on many traffic-light controlled junctions which incorporate pedestrian crossings does not allow sufficient time for right turning drivers.

For example, if you need to wait for oncoming vehicles before you can clear the junction, the green man may come on and people start crossing. Look out for the pedestrians and when safe, pull forward and wait in front of the crossing until it is clear and you can proceed.

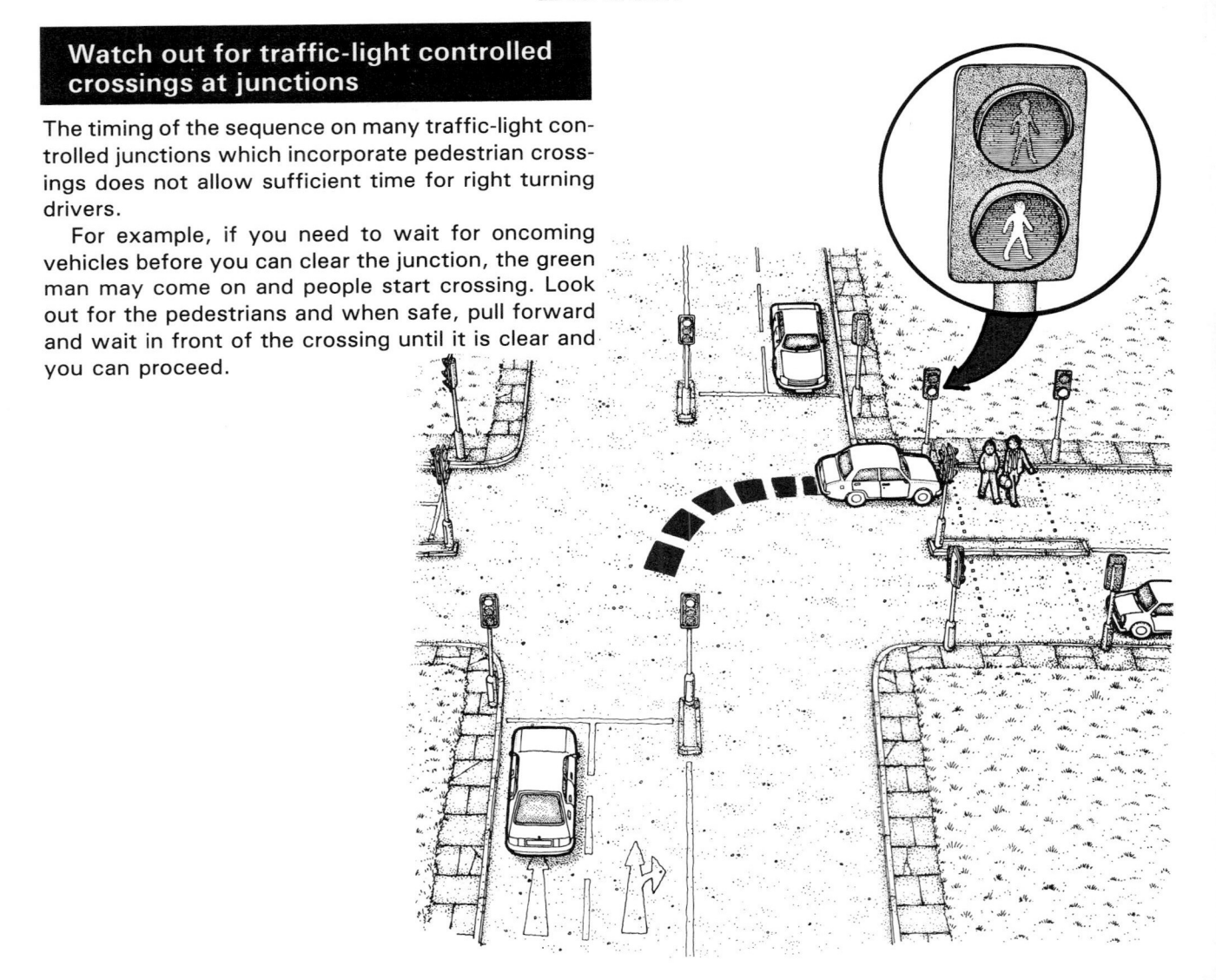

Is overtaking necessary and is it safe?

Before deciding to overtake, ask yourself if the benefit is worth the risk. There is little point if you are turning off soon after or if there is a line of traffic ahead.

Consider what the other driver may be doing. Will he pull out to pass a parked car or cyclist, or is he signalling to turn?

Last, but not least, is it safe behind? Is someone overtaking you?

Getting into position to see the way ahead before overtaking

To get a good view of the road ahead stay well back and first look along the nearside. Move over to look along the offside for a long, straight stretch of wide road free of oncoming vehicles, obstructions and side turns.

Engage a lower gear, usually 3rd if you are travelling below 50mph or 2nd below 20mph, and be ready to accelerate quickly.

After overtaking, pull back on to your own side as soon as you can do so without cutting in.

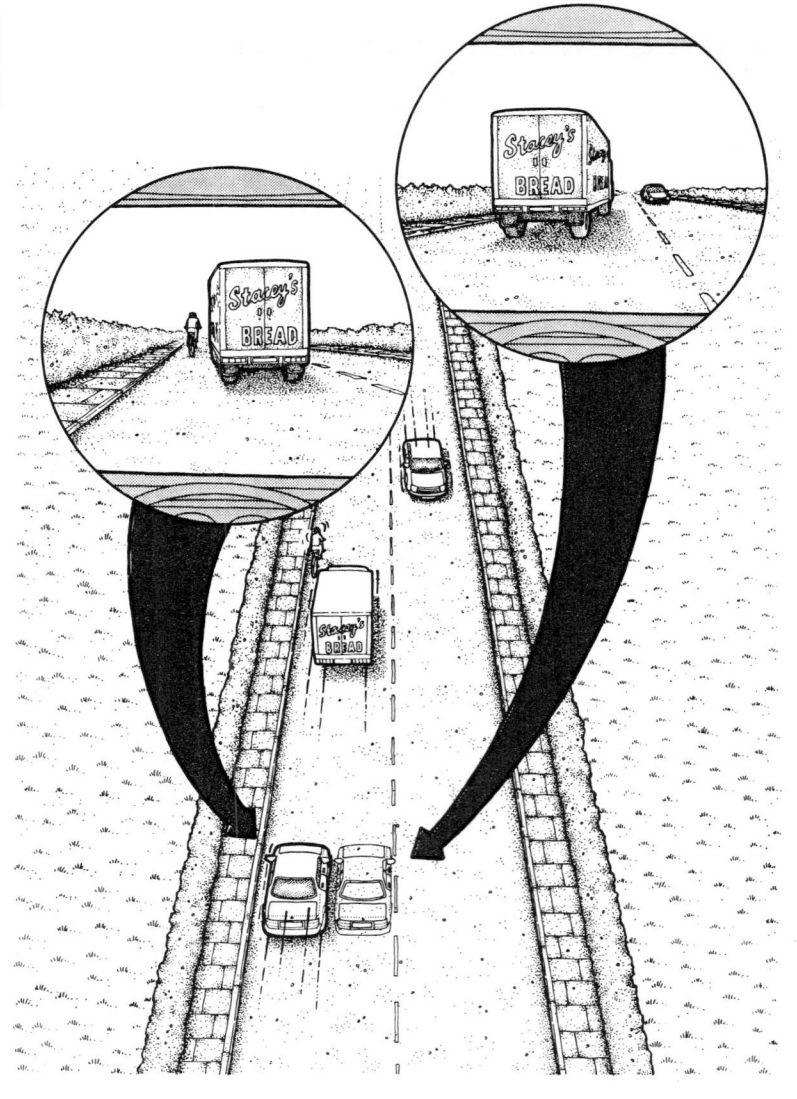

Situations in which you must not overtake

Think about the distance you will travel and also about the time you will need to overtake and get safely back in. Consider also the distance which will be covered by any oncoming vehicles.

Do not overtake where your view is restricted by bends or hill crests, or when you are approaching pedestrian crossings and side roads.

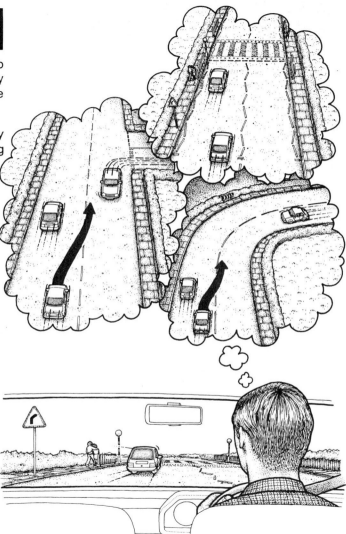

Stage 7

Checkpoint

1. Signals given at the wrong time:
   [a] can be dangerous.
   [b] may cause an overtaking driver to panic.
   [c] both [a] and [b].

2. On a multi-laned road, should you normally:
   [a] drive in the centre lane?
   [b] drive in the left-hand lane?
   [c] either [a] or [b]?

3. When driving straight ahead at a two-lane roundabout should you normally:
   [a] use the left lane?
   [b] use the right lane?

4. When leaving a roundabout, should you normally:
   [a] leave in the left lane?
   [b] leave in the right lane?

5. On finding yourself in the wrong lane at a junction, should you:
   [a] stay in it and miss your road?
   [b] pull up and wait until you can change?
   [c] signal and move over quickly?

6. When driving in lanes, should you:
   [a] position to the left of the lane?
   [b] position to the right of the lane?
   [c] position in the middle of the lane?

7. When driving in the right-hand lane of a one-way street, should you expect:
   [a] pedestrians walking into your path looking the other way?
   [b] other vehicles overtaking on your left?
   [c] both [a] and [b]?

8. The flashing amber light at a pelican crossing means:
   [a] give way to pedestrians on the crossing.
   [b] pedestrians waiting are allowed to start crossing.

9. Going straight on at a multi-laned crossroads, there is a parked car ahead. The right lane is held up by turning traffic. Would you:
   [a] approach in the left lane until you have passed the right turning traffic?
   [b] approach in the right-hand lane?

10. Going straight on at traffic-lights, you notice your exit is blocked, would you:
    [a] move into the junction and wait?
    [b] wait at the stop line?

11. When turning right at traffic-lights, should you normally:
    [a] give way to oncoming traffic?
    [b] wait at the stop line until there is a break in the on-coming traffic?

12. A green filter arrow means:
    [a] you may proceed in that direction only when the main light is on green.
    [b] you may proceed in that direction regardless of any other light showing.

13. The main danger when turning right is:
    [a] oncoming traffic.
    [b] other right turning traffic.

14. Arm signals are particularly recommended when:
    [a] taking a driving test.
    [b] passing parked cars.
    [c] giving way at pedestrian crossings.

15. Drivers must give precedence to pedestrians on:
    [a] zebra crossings.
    [b] the pavement by a pelican crossing when amber is flashing.

16. Where there is a refuge in the middle of a zebra crossing, should it be treated as:
    [a] one continuous crossing?
    [b] two separate crossings?

17. Dual carriageways are more dangerous than motorways because:
    [a] traffic travels faster.
    [b] traffic can turn right from them.
    [c] traffic can overtake on both sides.

18. When crossing a dual carriageway should you:
    [a] wait until it is safe to drive across both sides in one movement?
    [b] treat each side as a separate road and stop in the middle?
    [c] either [a] or [b] depending upon the width of the central reserve and the flow of traffic?

Checkpoint answers

1. [c] 2. [b] 3. [a] 4. [a] 5. [a] 6. [c]
7. [c] 8. [a] 9. [a] 10. [b] 11. [a] 12. [b]
13. [a] 14. [c] 15. [a] 16. [b] 17. [b] 18. [c]

How to Avoid Accidents

Introduction

Road accidents currently claim over 5,000 lives, maim over 250,000 people and cost the UK over £2 thousand million every year. Fourteen lives are lost and 685 people are seriously injured every day. The cost alone is £230,000 for every hour of every day.

It has been shown that systematic training techniques can reduce these accidents by as much as 50 per cent.

This lesson is the final preparation leading up to your driving test. Before starting it you should feel confident about controlling your car and driving in traffic. You will have dealt with most types of hazard and feel competent to carry out your reversing exercises and other manoeuvres. You will be almost at driving test standard.

By now you will have discovered for yourself that other drivers and road users make mistakes. This lesson teaches you how to deal with them. It shows you some of the ways that experienced drivers learn to avoid accidents by compensating for the mistakes of others.

Before going out to practise you should first learn the Highway Code rules listed below. Work through the lesson and complete the checkpoint before going out on the road.

Rule	55	Fog code.
Rules	66-67	Pedestrians.
Rules	130-131	Parking at night.

You should also study the speed limit chart on page 48 with particular reference to driving a motor car.

Facing the consequences of accidents

Accidents cost lives. They can prove very expensive and you could lose your driving licence.

No matter who is at fault, or whose right of way it may have been, a collision can cause injury, misery and a lot of inconvenience.

If ONLY I'd.....

Being responsible about speed

Try to be a responsible and caring driver. Be sensible and safe about where, and how, you use speed. When you double your speed, remember that your braking distance increases by four times.

Driving too fast does not just mean breaking the speed limit. There are many times when the legal limit can be dangerously fast. Some people think they are driving at a safe speed for the conditions when they are really going far too quickly. This is usually because they have poorly developed hazard recognition skills and are oblivious to the dangers which exist or the risks they are taking.

Stage

8

Anticipating mistakes of other road users

By now you should have realised that other road users can make silly mistakes. Can you recall any near misses you have had because someone did something unexpected or foolish. Experienced drivers learn to anticipate where such things are most likely to occur and adjust their speed before the incident arises. To survive on the roads you must learn to do the same.

As you drive along you must continually look ahead for things which may move into, or across, your path. Think about what will happen if an on-coming car turns into a side road by crossing in front of you, or if a cyclist pulls out of a driveway into your path.

Also look for obstructions in the road, such as a parked vehicle, which restrict your view. Where your view is restricted there is a risk of other road users moving into your path unseen. Consider what you will do if a pedestrian runs out and adjust your speed until you are sure you will be able to pull up.

Be tolerant towards those less skilful than yourself

How well have you learnt the Highway Code rules? A proper understanding of the procedures laid out in the Highway Code will help you become more confident. Knowledgeable and skilful drivers recognise danger sooner and react to it more quickly and decisively than the more timid. Confident drivers are more relaxed, more tolerant and less likely to be frustrated by the mistakes of others. They are less easily provoked by bad manners and less likely to respond aggressively.

Some drivers have the wrong attitude and do not see any need to obey or even learn the rules of the road. They are aggressive and quick to lose their tempers. These deficiencies are a major cause of road accidents. Be patient. Aggressive behaviour puts others, perhaps less skilful than yourself, under pressure and could force them into doing something they cannot control.

Such behaviour could, and does, kill.

Do not let drivers following too closely behind you force you into driving faster than you feel capable of. Driving more slowly will reduce any subsequent need for heavy braking and increase the safety margins involved.

Keep calm and do not let impatient drivers bully you into moving into a major road against your better judgement.

Stage

8

Do not help to make accidents happen

Most accidents are the consequence of a combination of mistakes. Remove any one of these and the accident can be avoided. Read how the accident shown here could be avoided by any one of the three drivers involved.

The driver turning into the main road is looking to his right for traffic and not expecting vehicles approaching on his side of the road. If this driver had looked both ways before emerging the accident would not have happened.

Some drivers seem not to care about safety and park anywhere it is convenient for them without consideration for others. Others care, but just do not think or do not know the rules. Vehicles parked near junctions restrict vision and put drivers on to the wrong side of the road. If the driver of the parked car had left his vehicle in a safer place the accident would have been avoided.

The driver moving out to pass the parked vehicle is travelling too fast because he has failed to consider the possibility of anyone emerging from the side road. If he had recognised the potential danger here and consequently slowed down he would have been able to stop and avoid the accident.

Excessive speed on the approach to potential accident situations is usually the result of poorly developed hazard recognition skills and contributes to many collisions.

Concentrate all the time you are driving

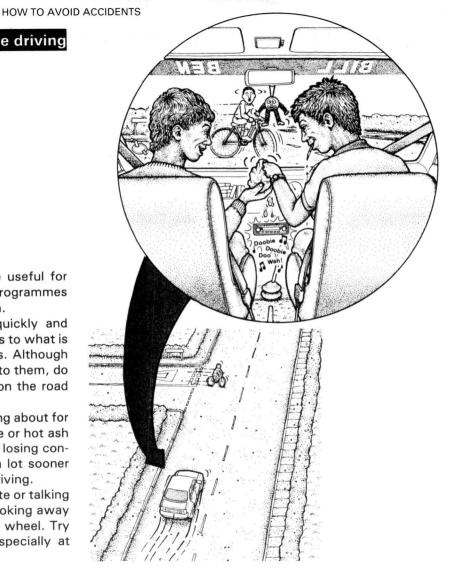

Concentrate on your driving. Radios are useful for road and weather reports and for light programmes but serious listening can be a distraction.

Traffic situations can change very quickly and conversation will lower your attentiveness to what is happening and slow down your reactions. Although it is polite to look at people when talking to them, do not do it while driving. Keep your eyes on the road ahead at all times.

Keep your hands on the wheel. Fumbling about for matches and lighters, a dropped cigarette or hot ash falling from a pipe could all result in your losing control of the car. Smoking could kill you a lot sooner than you may think if you do it while driving.

Tuning a radio, changing a tape cassette or talking into a CB radio microphone may mean looking away from the road with only one hand on the wheel. Try to avoid these things while moving, especially at speed, in traffic and on corners.

Stage 8

How to avoid accidents with oncoming vehicles

When driving concentrate all the time. Look out for potential danger ahead, such as an oncoming driver who may pull on to your side of the road in order to pass a stationary vehicle.

Work out in advance how this will affect you. Remember that traffic situations may change quickly. Think through how you might be affected by this.

Decide what you can do to reduce the risk. Will you need to hold back if the oncoming driver pulls on to your side of the road?

Look in your mirrors to find out what is behind and judge your approach speed and distance from the hazard. Be courteous yourself and acknowledge the courtesies extended to you by others.

Be prepared to slow down and compensate for the mistakes or deficiencies of others. Even though you may technically have the right of way, be ready to hold back and leave the other driver enough space to get through and back in again.

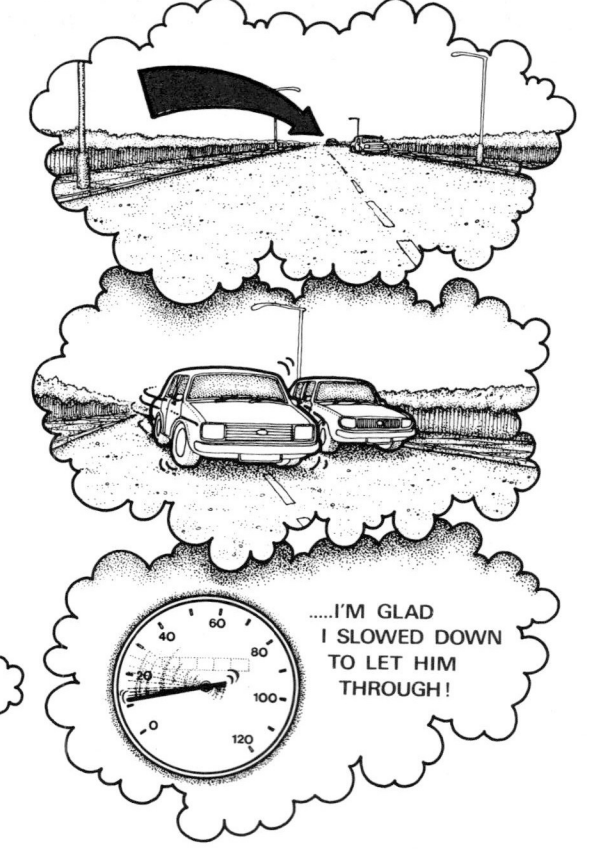

.....I'M GLAD I SLOWED DOWN TO LET HIM THROUGH!

How to avoid accidents with oncoming right turning vehicles

Watch out for oncoming drivers who are signalling to turn right across your path. If they are nearing their point of turn as you approach, make sure that they are holding back for you.

Look at the driver and try to make eye contact with him. Be on your guard if he is looking the other way as he may turn across your path.

Even though you may technically have right of way be prepared to slow down and hold back.

When driving straight on at traffic lights, watch out for oncoming drivers who are unable to see you because of the traffic waiting in the lane to your right.

How to avoid accidents with emerging vehicles

Approaching side roads, and in particular minor cross-roads, watch out for drivers approaching the give way lines too quickly to pull up. Be particularly careful, and slow down, where junctions may be hidden behind parked vehicles and where the emerging driver's view may be restricted. Where drivers are waiting to pull out of the junction try to make eye contact with them. This ensures they have seen you and reduces the risk of them moving out.

Even though you may technically have the right of way, be prepared to slow down and hold back.

Check your mirrors, cover your brake and approach the crossroad at a speed at which you can stop, or at least slow down, if someone pulls out.

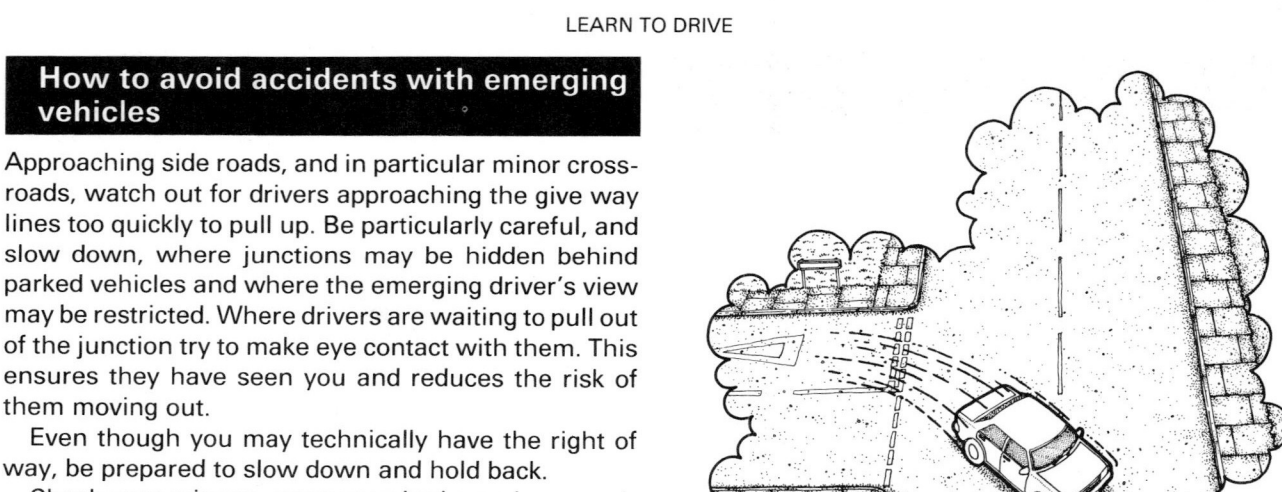

How to avoid accidents with vehicles to your sides

Stay well back from vehicles ahead which are travelling in lanes to your sides. Let them move into your lane to pass an obstruction in theirs. Avoid driving in the blind spots of other drivers who are just ahead of you.

Anticipate the actions of drivers needing to change lanes and in particular the drivers of large vehicles who may need to steer an unusual course through some junctions.

They may swing out before turning left or position as far to the left as they can when turning right into a factory entrance or narrow road.

Because of the size of their vehicle they often cut corners or take an unusual course through roundabouts.

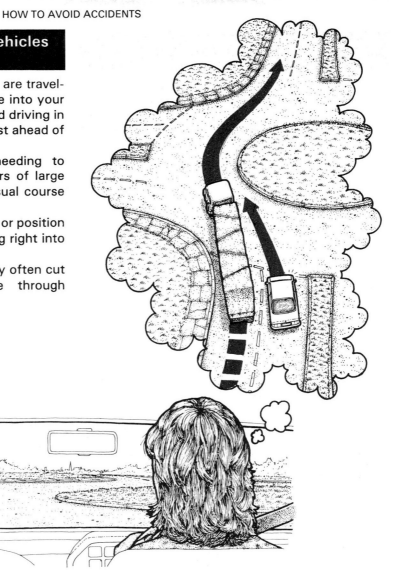

Stage

8

Leave enough space for the drivers of large vehicles to manoeuvre

When you see a large vehicle signalling to turn, hold well back and allow plenty of time and room for it to get round.

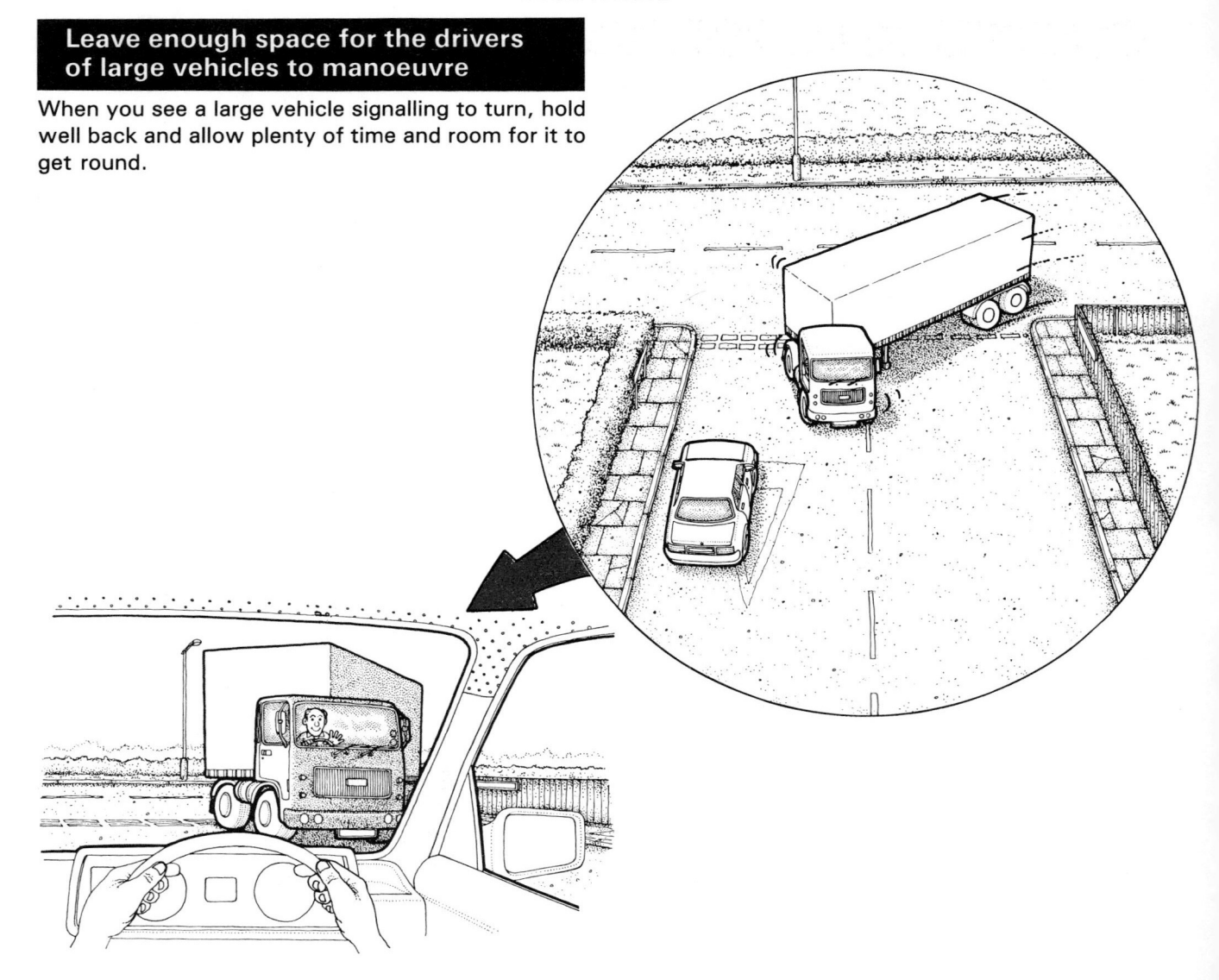

How to avoid accidents near buses and stationary vehicles

Bus drivers frequently stop to pick up or set down passengers. Many do this with little or no warning. Stay well back from them and watch out for signals or other signs that they may be pulling up at a bus stop; for example, where you can see people queueing at a bus stop or waiting at the bus door ready to get off.

If you think the bus is stopping try to keep in an overtaking position and get a clear view of the road ahead. Hold well back in this central position until you get a safe opportunity to pass.

If you are able to pass, remember your view is restricted. Be prepared to slow down and watch out for people moving into the road from behind the bus.

When coming up behind stationary buses watch out for the driver signalling to move away from the bus stop. Be prepared to give way where it is safe to do so, particularly when driving in towns.

Using the mirror to avoid accidents with overtaking vehicles

Use your mirrors frequently as you drive along to check for any vehicles that may be overtaking you, and allow them room to pull back in ahead of you.

Check the mirrors for those who may be overtaking as you prepare to turn. Be prepared to slow down, stop and let them go before you turn.

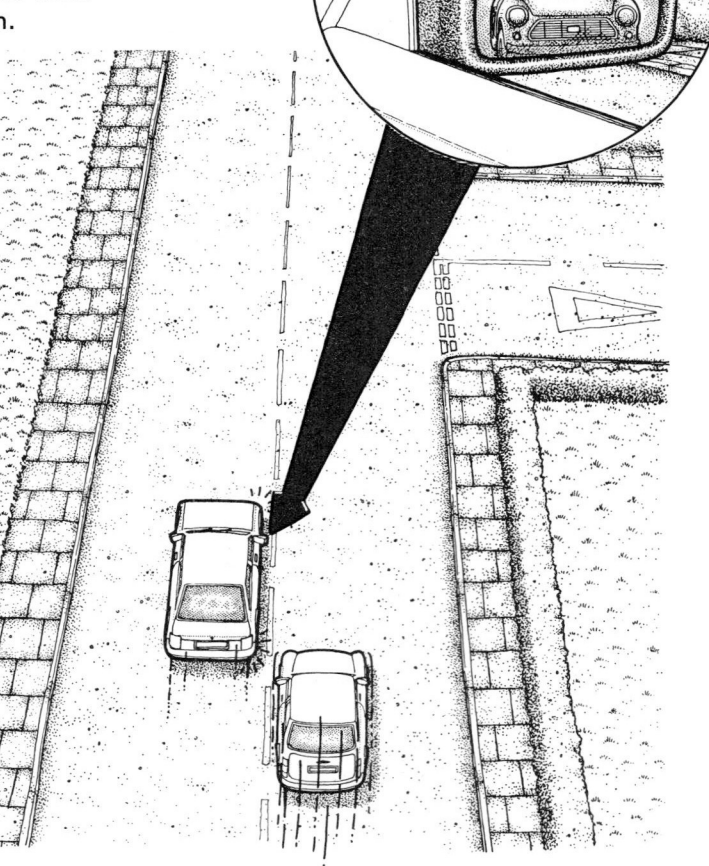

How to avoid accidents near bends and hill crests

Approaching bends or hill crests bear in mind that there may be a vehicle turning across your path, pedestrians in the road or a vehicle parked just out of sight. Be prepared to slow down to ensure you can stop well within the distance you can see to be clear.

Be constantly aware that there may be an oncoming vehicle moving towards you along your side of the road. Be prepared to hold back and give them time to return to their own side of the road.

How to avoid accidents near parked vehicles

When approaching parked vehicles look for signs of movement through the windows and for people stepping into the road. Watch for doors opening and people getting in or out. Expect other drivers to move out of side roads ahead of you as their view is also blocked by the parked vehicles.

Leave plenty of clearance when passing parked cars and watch out for people walking between them, particularly on your left side. Be prepared to slow down as you approach, and hold back for oncoming vehicles.

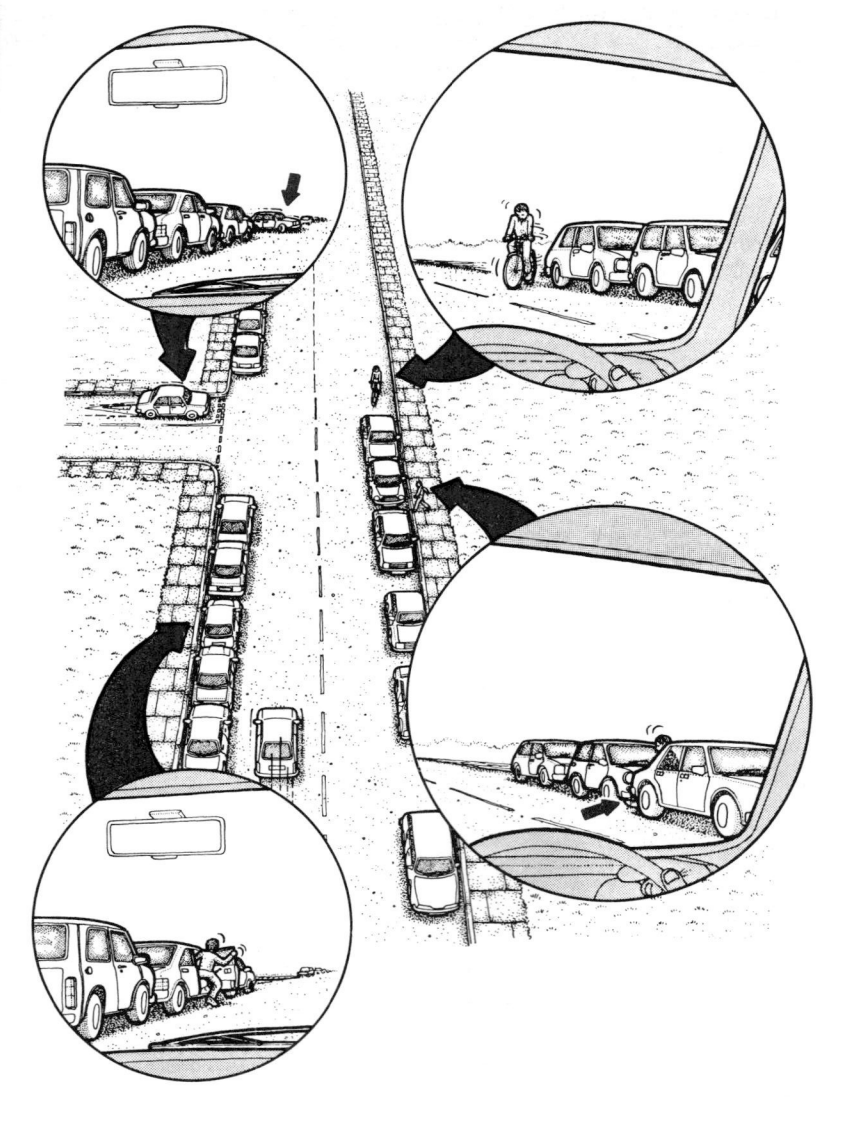

Care for the safety of pedestrians

Two out of every three pedestrians killed or seriously injured are either under 15 or over 60. The very young and old may sometimes misjudge the speed and distance of approaching vehicles. They can step out unexpectedly into the road.

Be patient with old people who tend to be slow and hesitant. Show extra care towards the disabled and infirm. Look out for blind people with white walking sticks or guide dogs. Remember too that some pedestrians who are hard of hearing or completely deaf may not hear your vehicle approaching.

Look out for pedestrians in or near the road at all times, but particularly when driving in shopping streets and when approaching junctions, corners and mobile shops. Also watch out for them walking out between parked or stationary vehicles.

Be prepared to slow down for pedestrians and drive with consideration for their feelings and proper care for their safety. Leave plenty of clearance when passing them and approach at a safe speed where they are walking in or near the road. Check your mirror and be ready to stop if necessary. Be prepared to sound your horn to warn them of your presence. Do this as a friendly warning and never as a reprimand.

If you are going along a busy shopping street drive more slowly and keep further away from the kerb. Where pedestrians are walking or standing close to the kerb check your mirrors and be prepared to move further out in the road as you approach them.

Drive slowly near schools, particularly at the times when children come and go. Be particularly careful near ice-cream vans and where you see very small children who are not restrained or holding someone's hand.

How to avoid accidents with pedestrians and children

When you want to cross a footpath, for example when turning into a drive or works' entrance, you must give way to any pedestrian walking on it.

When you are driving across the pavement out of a blind exit, be particularly careful and be prepared to sound your horn lightly.

If you have to reverse out, even more care will be required. Check that there are no pedestrians around before you start. Move slowly backwards and keep looking out for them all the time.

Children tend to be impulsive and can move very quickly and unexpectedly. They are usually too busy playing to notice what you are doing.

Check on following traffic and approach them slowly. Be prepared to stop.

Avoiding accidents with people walking in the road

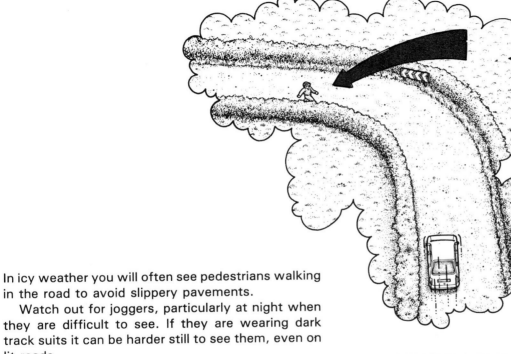

In icy weather you will often see pedestrians walking in the road to avoid slippery pavements.

Watch out for joggers, particularly at night when they are difficult to see. If they are wearing dark track suits it can be harder still to see them, even on lit roads.

Expect to meet people walking in, or crossing, the road ahead and just out of sight when you are travelling round bends or over hill crests, and especially on country roads with no footpaths.

Check on following traffic and be prepared to slow down. Be ready to pull up if necessary or to move round them.

How to avoid accidents with cyclists

Give cyclists plenty of clearance. The closer you get to them the more they may seem to wobble. When you are unable to pass them, slow down and keep in an overtaking position staying well back until you are sure you can get by safely. Allow extra room for them, particularly when they are pedalling uphill or steering round roadside grates or potholes.

Watch out for cyclists riding along close to the kerb when you are emerging from road junctions, particularly at night, in poor daylight and when it is raining.

Be patient and allow even more space for children on bicycles. Very young ones sometimes signal one way but then turn the other. Hold back if you sense they may behave unpredictably.

Some cyclists may ride along on the wrong side of the road towards you or pull straight out of junctions, without looking.

Also watch out for children playing and performing unusual actions like 'wheelies' with their bicycles.

Anticipate cyclists pulling out round stationary vehicles

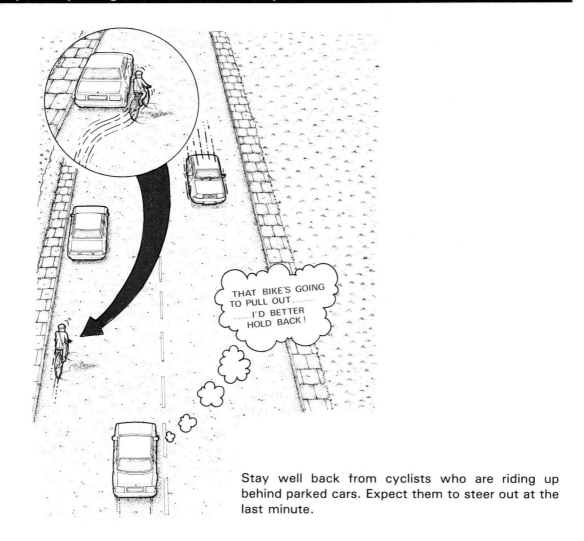

THAT BIKE'S GOING TO PULL OUT........ ......I'D BETTER HOLD BACK!

Stay well back from cyclists who are riding up behind parked cars. Expect them to steer out at the last minute.

Using the mirror to avoid accidents with cyclists and motorcyclists

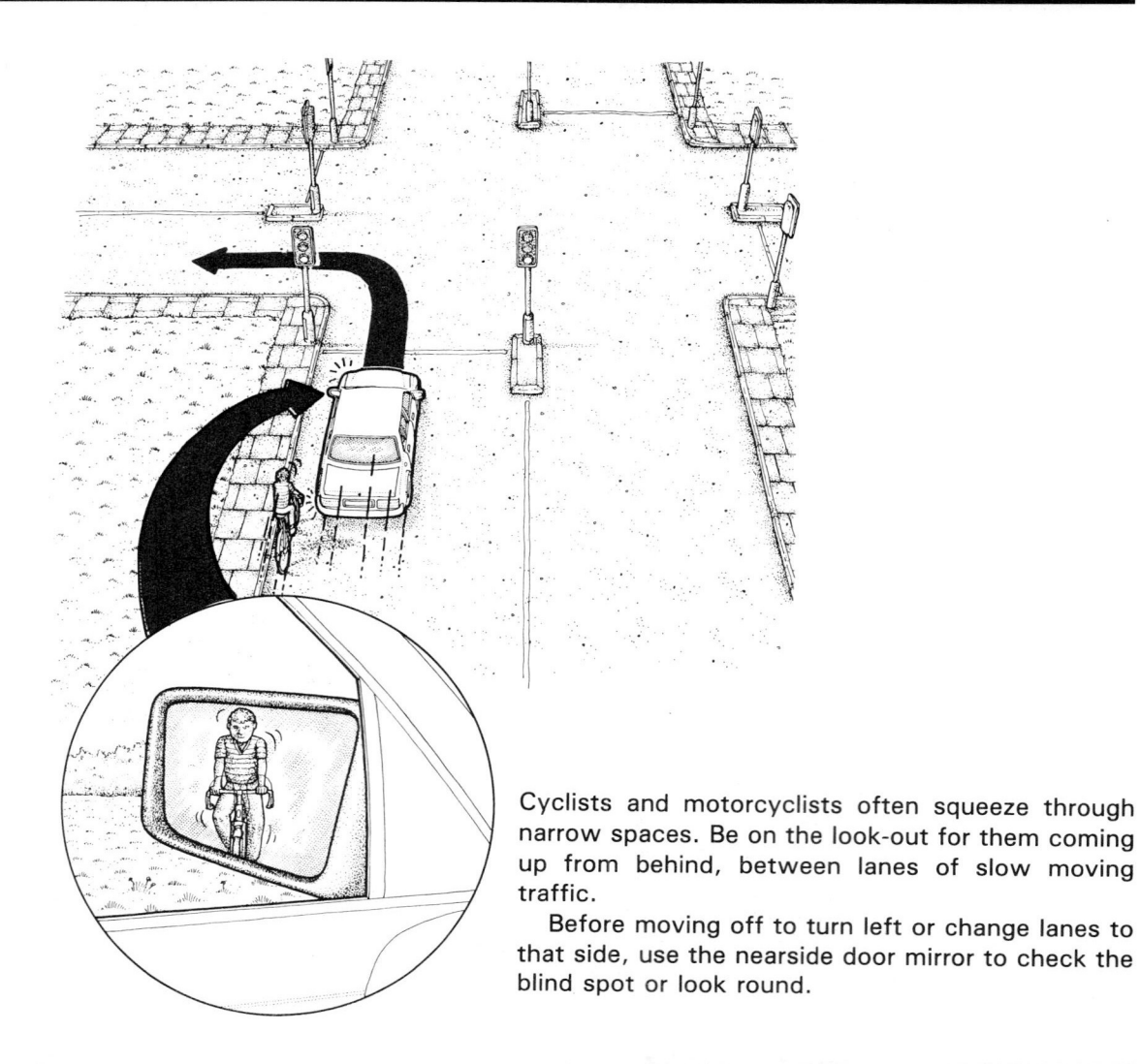

Cyclists and motorcyclists often squeeze through narrow spaces. Be on the look-out for them coming up from behind, between lanes of slow moving traffic.

Before moving off to turn left or change lanes to that side, use the nearside door mirror to check the blind spot or look round.

How to avoid accidents with animals

Anticipate the unpredictable behaviour of animals. Look out for dogs off leads, keep a check on following traffic and be prepared to slow down. If a dog runs out in front of you keep both hands on the wheel, hold the steering on a straight course and brake firmly. Slow down when approaching horses and hold well back until you can leave enough room to pass them safely. Avoid passing at speed, with a high revving engine, and do not use the horn.

Beware of
Cats and Dogs

Stage

8

How to avoid accidents on country roads

When driving at higher speeds on the open road concentrate hard and plan ahead. Keep a firmer grip on the wheel and drive a little further out from the side of the road.

The countryside holds its own dangers. Drive slowly on narrow roads, through villages and near farm entrances. Take extra care at lambing time and when driving in country parks. Be patient when driving behind slow-moving vehicles on narrow roads where it is unsafe to overtake. Expect sharp bends, mud on the road and agricultural vehicles pulling out into your path from fields and farm yards. Go slowly where your view is restricted. Expect to find obstructions in the road, slower moving traffic, and pedestrians walking in the road.

Make sure that others can see you

Make sure that other drivers can see you at night and in poor daylight conditions by using dipped headlights. Use them in fog, heavy rain and snow.

IT'S EASIER TO SEE CARS WITH HEADLIGHTS ON IN THESE CONDITIONS...... I WONDER IF THOSE WHO ONLY USE SIDELIGHTS REALISE HOW DIFFICULT THEY ARE TO SEE......

How to avoid accidents when driving in the dark

At night your view is often masked by shadows. Drive more slowly. Watch out for pedestrians who may be difficult to see if they are wearing dark clothing. Look out for cyclists who may be riding without lights.

Dip your headlights and do not dazzle the drivers of oncoming vehicles or the driver of the vehicle in front of you.

How to avoid accidents when driving in fog

Avoid parking on the road in fog.

Drive slowly so that you can stop within the distance you can see to be clear. Keep your windows free of condensation and watch out for obstructions in the road.

Use your ears and listen for other traffic before moving out of junctions. Remember that some other drivers may not have their headlights on.

Anticipate the effects of strong side winds

Expect strong side winds when you are driving in high, exposed places or on bridges. Hold the steering wheel firmly and be ready to compensate for the wind deflecting you from your course when you are overtaking high-sided vehicles. Remember that those in the lanes to your sides will also be affected. Allow extra clearance when passing cyclists in these conditions.

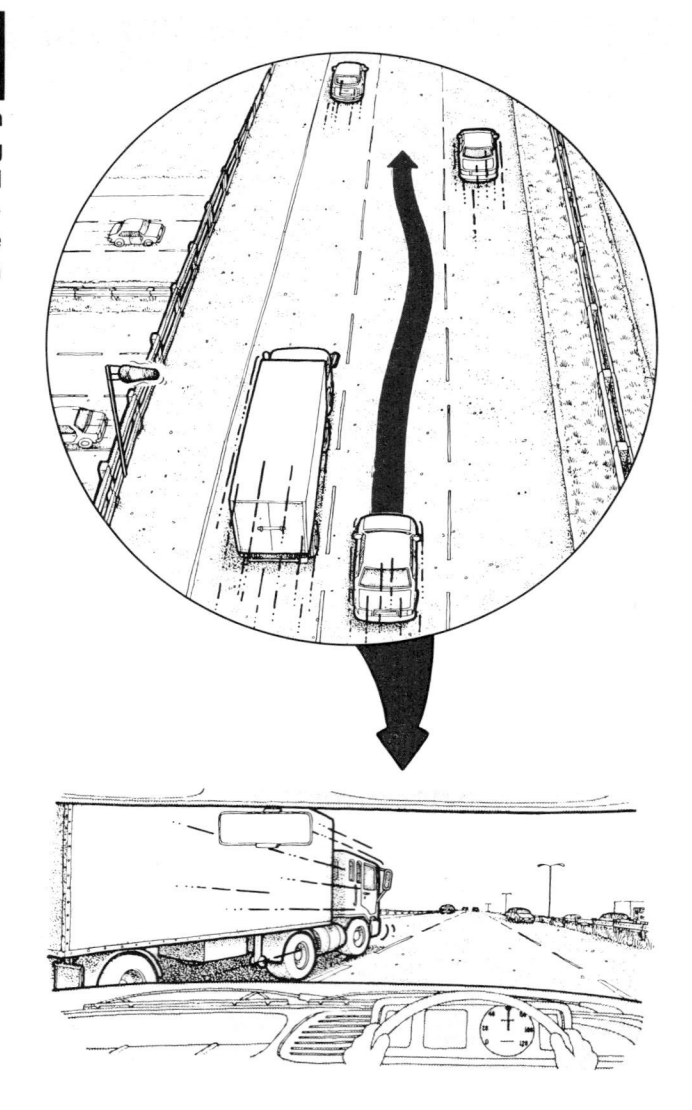

How to avoid skids - Part 1

Skids are most often caused by harsh acceleration, braking and steering, frequently combined with excessive speed. Averting the circumstances which lead to these is the most effective way of preventing them. To do this you must look well ahead, see the dangers and act early enough to avoid excessive pedal pressures and sudden steering movements. For example, a driver who slows down early, particularly in wet weather, after sighting a group of children near the kerb edge, will need less braking pressure if one of them dashes into the road.

Concentrate all the time and stay alert while you are driving. Look ahead, anticipate the possible actions of others. Be prepared to slow down early. Use the brakes and accelerator progressively and avoid unnecessary journeys in bad weather.

In snow and ice slow down early with light braking pressure. Gentle braking is less likely to cause skidding than changing into a lower gear. Use gradual acceleration and keep in the highest gear possible without distressing the engine. When going uphill in snow try to maintain a steady momentum by staying well back from the vehicle ahead.

Stage 8

How to avoid skids – Part 2

Avoid accelerating or braking on bridges in freezing temperatures as black ice forms on these first.

Read the road surface conditions ahead and slow down well before reaching any bumpy parts of the road, particularly where the edges are rough or broken.

Keep off soft verges and avoid heavy braking on loose gravel or when the road surface is wet or muddy. The combination of oil, rubber, dust and water makes the road very slippery after a long dry spell followed by light summer showers. Damp patches on the road under trees are likely to be very greasy.

....MUST DRIVE SLOWER AND BRAKE GENTLY

How to avoid aquaplaning

To avoid aquaplaning replace worn tyres and drive more slowly on wet road surfaces.

A water cushion will build up in front of fast moving tyres. If they are unable to displace this, the tyres ride up on to it and lose surface contact. The driver then loses control.

With new tyres aquaplaning can occur at less than 60mph. With worn tyres it can occur at much lower speeds.

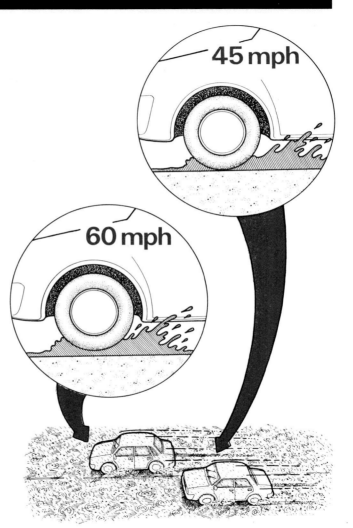

Stage

8

How to correct a skid

There are skid pans at various locations throughout the country where drivers can receive proper instruction and controlled practice in the techniques used to correct skids. Ask at your local police station, your road safety officer at the county offices, or at one of the motoring organisations for details of skid pans in your area. Some driving schools also give lessons in skid correction.

The most common skids are caused by braking too hard and by sudden steering movement at excessive speeds. Braking too hard may cause the wheels to stop turning. If this happens the car will slide further along the road. An effective remedy is to release the brake and reapply it in a rapid on-off, on-off action.

Attempts to steer round a bend at an excessive speed, particularly in wet conditions, may result in the rear of the car sliding away from the centre of the corner. This rear wheel skid is the most common type and is easily recognised because the car goes off course. Your natural reaction should be to steer back on course, but do not over-react. If the rear swings to the right you should steer right; if it swings to the left, steer left.

Checkpoint

1. When driving in fog you should:

   [a] follow the tail lights of the vehicle ahead.
   [b] use dipped headlights.

2. When driving in fog you should:

   [a] allow extra time for the journey.
   [b] clean the windows, lights and reflectors.
   [c] both [a] and [b].

3. Drivers should give way to pedestrians:

   [a] crossing roads they are turning into.
   [b] when emerging from property bordering the road.
   [c] both [a] and [b].

4. When driving past animals should you:

   [a] be ready to stop?
   [b] sound your horn?
   [c] drive past quickly?

5. Parking on a road at night:

   [a] should be avoided.
   [b] is illegal.

6. On a two lane road something falls from your car. Should you normally:

   [a] stop as soon as you can safely do so?
   [b] remove the article from the carriageway?
   [c] both [a] and [b]?

7. If you are first to arrive at the scene of an accident, should you first of all:

   [a] warn other traffic?
   [b] get uninjured people out of the vehicles?

8. Staying well back from a slow-moving vehicle:

   [a] gives a better view.
   [b] helps anticipate its actions.
   [c] both [a] and [b].

9. Drivers should normally give way to:

   [a] buses signalling to move out from bus stops on country roads.
   [b] buses signalling to move out from bus stops in towns.

10. Approaching a blind bend, should you expect:

    [a] pedestrians in the road just out of sight?
    [b] oncoming vehicles moving along your side of the road?
    [c] both [a] and [b]?

11. The road surface can be very slippery:

    [a] after a light summer shower.
    [b] in damp patches under the shade of trees.
    [c] both [a] and [b].

12. Wind will affect your vehicle when:

    [a] driving in exposed places.
    [b] passing high-sided vehicles.
    [c] both [a] and [b].

13. Driving errors are caused by:

    [a] bad temper.
    [b] lack of concentration.
    [c] both [a] and [b].

14. When waiting to emerge from a busy junction, the driver behind sounds his horn. Would you:

    [a] pull out of the junction quickly?
    [b] keep calm and make up your own mind?

15. Drivers should look for pedestrians:

    [a] near corners and junctions.
    [b] before reversing out of driveways.
    [c] both [a] and [b].

Checkpoint answers

1. [b] **2.** [c] **3.** [c] **4.** [a] **5.** [a]

6. [c] **7.** [a] **8.** [c] **9.** [b] **10.** [c]

11. [c] **12.** [c] **13.** [c] **14.** [b] **15.** [c]

Stage

8

133

How to Pass Your Driving Test

Introduction

Before going for your test make sure you have studied the official Department of Transport book, 'Your Driving Test'. You should be able to get one of these from your driving instructor or any good book shop.

Learn 'The law's demands' (the last few pages in the Highway Code) and make sure you cover the following areas for drivers of motor vehicles:

- Before driving make sure that . . .
- When driving you must/must not . . .
- When you stop you must/must not . . .
- If you are involved in an accident you must . . .
- When motorway driving you must/must not . . .

Learn 'First aid on the road' and 'Vehicle security'. You will find both of these at the end of the Highway Code.

Read through the lesson carefully before your instructor carries out your first mock test. This will usually be about six weeks before the official appointment. If you have followed the advice given in this guide and you have listened to your instructor and practised sufficiently you should have no difficulty in passing your test.

Before the test

Make sure you are well prepared for the test. If you have studied the Highway Code properly, followed the course instructions and had enough practice, you should pass quite easily. Do not worry about feeling anxious as this will help to keep you alert.

As the date gets nearer, your instructor will give you a couple of mock tests. These show you what to expect and help to settle your nerves. If you feel over-anxious and make lots of mistakes on these, it is a sure indication that you should get more practice before taking the real thing.

Arrive at the test centre in time to park your car and go into the waiting room two or three minutes early. Tell your instructor in plenty of time if you wish to go to the toilet as facilities are not always available at the centres. If you need an interpreter or want your instructor to sit in on the test, just tell the examiner. He or she will not object.

Examiners understand what it is like to be tested and are frequently checked by having senior examiners sitting in on tests. If this happens on your test just forget it, concentrate, and get on with your driving.

First, the examiner will ask you to sign a form and enquire if you have any disabilities not declared on your application. Once this is over you will be asked to read a number plate after which the examiner invites you to get into your car. Check it is safe to walk into the road, get in and get comfortable.

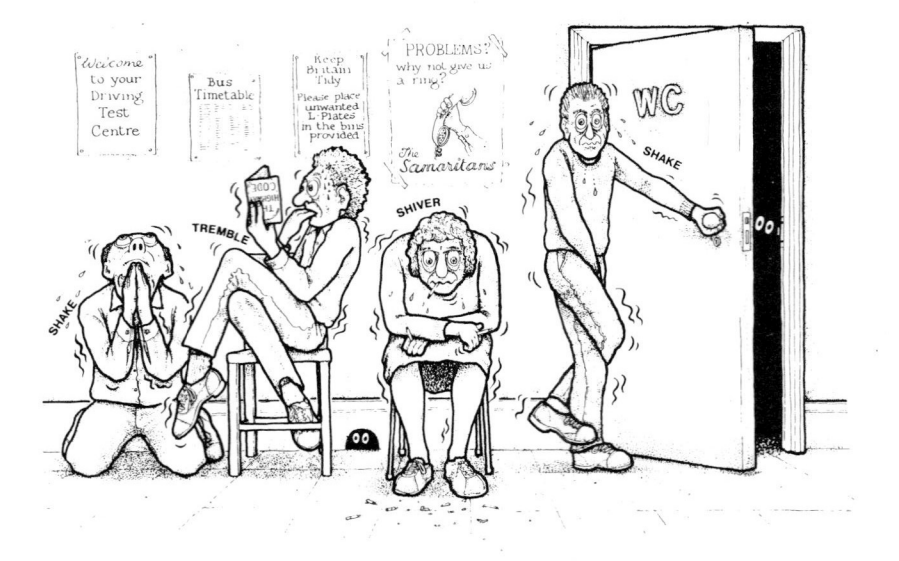

On the test

Once beside you the examiner will tell you to follow the road ahead unless he tells you to turn or you are directed otherwise by road signs. He will not try to trick you into doing something you should not and will give you plenty of warning for turns. Watch out for signs and act on them. Ask the examiner to repeat a direction if you are not sure about it.

The first part of the test is a fairly straightforward drive which gives you time to settle down. Your nerves should soon disappear once you get going.

Try to have confidence in the examiner and concentrate on your driving or you may worry more about what he is thinking than on what you are doing.

Keep within the speed limits but do not try to impress the examiner by driving extra slowly. Examiners are not fooled by artificial over-cautiousness. If in doubt you should always hold back, but try to drive at normal speeds, making safe progress at junctions and in traffic.

Stage

9

Look well ahead to steer and plan your course. Concentrate on what you must do to deal with each situation as it arises. Adjust your speed before reaching any traffic hold-ups, junctions and places where your view is restricted. Allow adequate clearance and safety margins and anticipate the actions of other road users moving into or across your path. Use your mirrors frequently and act sensibly on what is happening behind you.

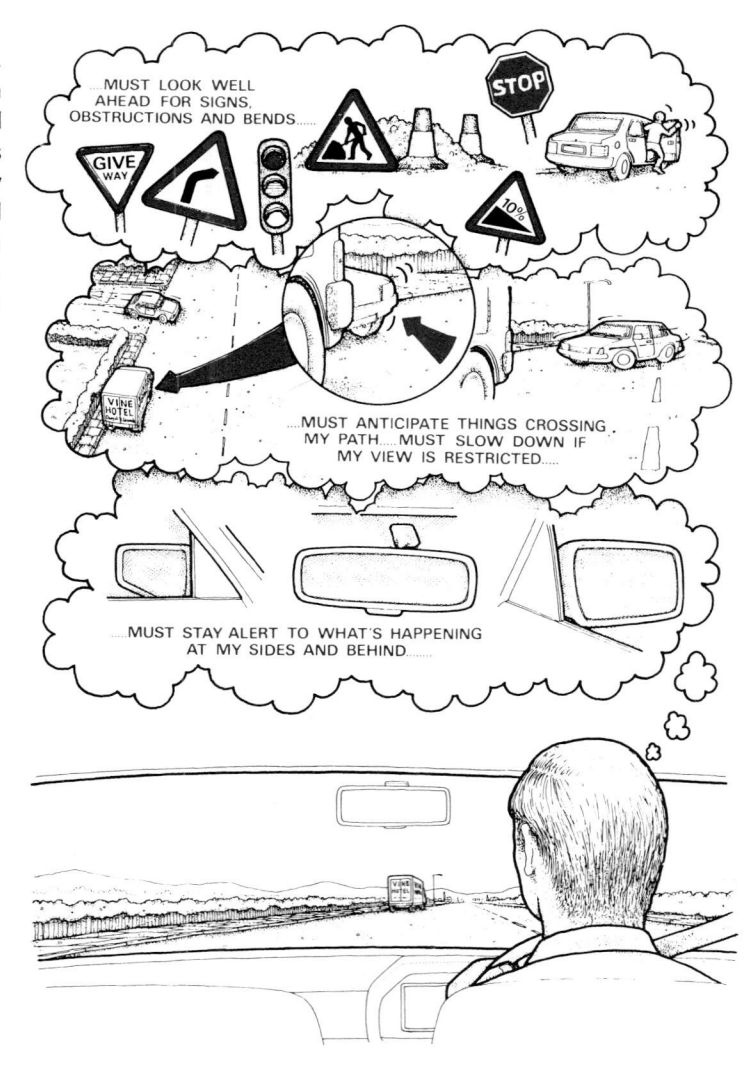

The examiner will ask you to pull up at a convenient place on the left several times during your test. Do not worry about this, it is only to give you further instructions. Remember, it is your responsibility each time to select a safe and legal position for stopping. When asked to pull up just behind a parked vehicle, make sure you leave room for moving off again.

The first special exercise you will be asked to carry out is the emergency stop. You will be asked to pull up as if a child has run out in front of you. The examiner will explain the signal for stopping and ask you to drive on again. Keep calm and use your mirror frequently as you drive along. When the signal is given, react promptly and stop quickly but under full control.

The next special exercise will be reversing into a side road. You will be asked to pull up just before a corner where the examiner will give you the instructions for the exercise. If your path into the side road is obstructed in any way, tell the examiner. He or she will not mind and will find you another corner. If you find yourself going wide or getting too close to the kerb, stop. Pull forwards and start again before it gets too late and becomes a serious fault.

The final exercise is turning the car round in the road between the two kerbs. Again, the examiner will ask you to pull up on the left. You can usually tell why the examiner is asking you to pull up from the nature of the road. Park away from other vehicles and kerbside hazards such as trees and lamp posts. Should you find there are obstructions at the kerbside when asked to do this exercise, be prepared to move away from them before starting the exercise. The examiner will not mind.

On returning to the test centre, the examiner will ask you questions on the Highway Code and other motoring matters. These include identifying pictures of road signs and answering questions on topics such as skidding, parking, vehicle condition and motorways. You may also be asked about situations which arose during the test. Examiners will not expect you to recite answers parrot-fashion. All you need to do is give commonsense replies and show you understand the rules and principles. Although arm signals are no longer a specific part of the test you may be asked to demonstrate them at the end.

Good luck!

Stage

9

After passing the driving test

If you follow your instructor's advice we feel sure you will be one of the 750,000 successful candidates out of the 2,000,000 tests conducted each year. We hope you will continue to drive to, and strive to improve upon, the high standard needed to pass. Why not take an advanced test in the near future? Details are available from the Institute of Advanced Motorists, IAM House, 359 Chiswick High Road, London W4 4HS (01-994 4403) or RoSPA Advanced Drivers Association, Cannon House, The Priory Queensway, Birmingham B4 6BS (021-233 2461).

If you have failed the test

Over 1,000,000 people fail every year and we know and sympathise with how they must feel. The progress and revision chart following this chapter is linked to the Department of Transport syllabus. Use this to find the appropriate pages in the guide which relate to the faults marked on the failure form. The chart should assist your understanding of these points and help you to correct them. It provides you with a quick and simple reference to what you must revise and learn to do before taking your test again.

Checkpoint

1. The main items inspected on an MOT vehicle check are:

   [a] engine, gearbox, brakes and tyres.
   [b] brakes, lights, steering and tyres.
   [c] engine, body, brakes and tyres.

2. Engine oil level should normally be checked:

   [a] before every journey.
   [b] at least once a week.
   [c] only at main service intervals.

3. Lights and indicators should be checked:

   [a] every day.
   [b] once a week.
   [c] only at main service intervals.

4. At least once a week, drivers should check:

   [a] radiator coolant level.
   [b] windscreen washer liquid level.
   [c] both [a] and [b].

5. Skidding is caused by the:

   [a] driver.
   [b] weather conditions.
   [c] road surface condition.

6. A main cause of skidding is:

   [a] excessive speed for the conditions.
   [b] weather conditions.
   [c] road surface conditions.

7. If the rear of your car was skidding to the left, would you:

   [a] steer right?
   [b] steer left?
   [c] hold the wheel still?

8. During an emergency stop your wheels lock and skid, would you:

   [a] release the brake?
   [b] release the brake and then re-apply it?

9. Tyres must be:

   [a] correctly inflated.
   [b] free of cuts and defects.
   [c] both [a] and [b].

10. Tyres must have a minimum tread of:

    [a] 1 mm.
    [b] 1 ½ mm.
    [c] 2 mm.

11. You may cross the stop line on amber if:

    [a] you are too close to stop safely.
    [b] you can see no one is coming.
    [c] neither [a] nor [b].

12. At traffic lights you may proceed on amber if:

    [a] you have already crossed the stop line.
    [b] you can get across the junction before the other lights change.
    [c] neither [a] nor [b].

13. At a pelican crossing flashing amber means:

    [a] give way to pedestrians waiting to cross.
    [b] give way to pedestrians already crossing.
    [c] neither [a] nor [b].

14. When flashing amber is showing you should:

    [a] proceed if no one is on the crossing.
    [b] give way to pedestrians waiting to cross.
    [c] both [a] and [b].

15. At zebra crossings special consideration should be given to:

    [a] the old and the young.
    [b] people with prams.
    [c] both [a] and [b].

16. A white stick with two red bands means:

    [a] the pedestrian is deaf and dumb.
    [b] the pedestrian is deaf and blind.
    [c] either [a] or [b].

17. Driving past a row of parked vehicles should you look out for:

    [a] pedestrians walking out from between them?
    [b] car doors opening?
    [c] both [a] and [b]?

18. Driving past a row of parked vehicles should you look out for:

[a] drivers moving off without looking?
[b] cars emerging from hidden junctions?
[c] both [a] and [b]?

19. Where pedestrians are crossing the end of a road into which you are turning should you:

[a] sound your horn?
[b] give way to them?
[c] neither [a] nor [b]?

20. Approaching the end of a road should you:

[a] hold back for pedestrians crossing?
[b] make the pedestrians wait for you?
[c] sound your horn?

21. You may sound your horn when stationary if:

[a] you are testing it.
[b] you are in danger from a moving vehicle.
[c] both [a] and [b].

22. You should not sound your horn in a built-up area:

[a] between 7.30 pm and 11.00 am.
[b] between 10.00 pm and 10.00 am.
[c] between 11.30 pm and 7.00 am.

23. If another driver makes a mistake should you:

[a] flash your lights and sound your horn?
[b] keep cool and do not react angrily?
[c] neither [a] nor [b]?

24. Two continuous white lines along the centre of the road mean:

[a] no overtaking.
[b] do not cross or straddle the lines.
[c] no overtaking or crossing the lines.

25. A broken yellow line along the edge of the road means:

[a] no waiting at any time.
[b] waiting is limited to the times stated.
[c] no waiting at weekends.

26. You may stop and wait in a box junction if:

[a] you are prevented from turning right only by oncoming traffic.
[b] your exit straight ahead is blocked.
[c] your exit to the right is blocked.

27. Overtaking is not allowed when:

[a] driving on two-lane highways.
[b] driving in a built-up area.
[c] approaching pedestrian crossings.

28. Countdown markers are found:

[a] approaching the exits from motorways.
[b] approaching some roundabouts.
[c] both [a] and [b].

29. Countdown markers on motorways are:

[a] blue and white.
[b] green and white.
[c] black and white.

30. Countdown markers approaching roundabouts are:

[a] blue and white.
[b] green and white.
[c] black and white.

31. Countdown markers may indicate:

[a] the distance to a motorway exit.
[b] the distance to a hazard.
[c] both [a] or [b].

32. Round signs usually give:

[a] orders.
[b] warnings.
[c] information.

33. Triangular signs usually give:

[a] orders.
[b] warnings.
[c] information.

34. Red circles usually tell you:

[a] not to do something.
[b] to do something.
[c] neither [a] nor [b].

Stage

9

35. Blue circles usually tell you:

[a] not to do something.
[b] to do something.
[c] neither [a] nor [b].

36. At a mini roundabout, you should:

[a] give way to traffic from the right.
[b] give way to all traffic.
[c] neither [a] nor [b].

37. At a stop line you must:

[a] stop at the line.
[b] give way to traffic on the main road.
[c] both [a] and [b].

38. The routine sequence for overtaking is:

[a] mirror, signal, manoeuvre, position, speed, look.
[b] position, speed, look, mirror, signal, manoeuvre.
[c] mirror, signal, position, speed, look.

39. Driving in fog should you use:

[a] headlights on full beam?
[b] sidelights?
[c] headlights on dipped beam?

40. If dazzled by someone's lights should you:

[a] switch off your lights?
[b] flash your headlights?
[c] slow down or stop?

41. Following another vehicle at night should you:

[a] use dipped headlights?
[b] keep your lights on full beam to be seen?
[c] use sidelights only?

42. The overall stopping distance at 40mph is:

[a] 75 feet.
[b] 120 feet.
[c] 175 feet.

43. The overall stopping distance at 70mph is:

[a] 175 feet.
[b] 240 feet.
[c] 315 feet.

44. The recommended following distance is:

[a] two seconds.
[b] one yard for every mile per hour of speed.
[c] either [a] or [b].

45. If something falls from your car on a motorway should you:

[a] stop and retrieve it?
[b] pull up on the hard shoulder and phone the police?
[c] drive off the motorway at the first exit and contact the police?

46. The biggest cause of driving test failure is:

[a] taking it before being properly prepared.
[b] nerves.
[c] neither [a] nor [b].

47. Driving test examiners pass:

[a] a specified number of people each week.
[b] everyone who reaches the required standard.
[c] a specified number of people who reach the required standard each week.

48. Driving examiners expect test candidates to:

[a] act like learner drivers.
[b] drive safely and sensibly.
[c] drive perfectly.

49. Driving examiners:

[a] are strict and do not speak.
[b] try to put you at ease.
[c] neither [a] nor [b].

50. On a driving test you should:

[a] be positive and think of the things you should do to safely deal with situations
[b] drive extra slowly to show the examiner how careful you can be.
[c] think about all the things you should not do when driving.

143

Stage

9

Checkpoint answers

1. [b]   2. [b]   3. [a]   4. [c]   5. [a]   6. [a]

7. [b]   8. [b]   9. [c]   10. [a]   11. [a]   12. [a]

13. [b]   14. [a]   15. [c]   16. [b]   17. [c]   18. [c]

19. [b]   20. [a]   21. [b]   22. [c]   23. [b]   24. [b]

25. [b]   26. [a]   27. [c]   28. [c]   29. [a]   30. [b]

31. [c]   32. [a]   33. [b]   34. [a]   35. [b]   36. [a]

37. [a]   38. [b]   39. [c]   40. [c]   41. [a]   42. [b]

43. [c]   44. [c]   45. [b]   46. [a]   47. [b]   48. [b]

49. [b]   50. [a]

Progress Record and Driving Test Analysis

Use the following list and page references to help you organise your revision:

1. Read a number plate.
    -page 15

2. Attitude to and observance of Highway Code rules.
    -pages105, 106, 107, 125, 127, 128, 129, 130, 131, 132, 139, 150, 151

3. Take proper precautions before starting the engine.
    -page 28

4. Make proper use of:

    (i)   accelerator
          -pages 28, 41

    (ii) clutch
          -pages 26, 27, 40, 41

    (iii) gears
          -pages 24, 25, 33, 42

    (iv) footbrake
          -pages 28, 37, 42, 43

    (v)   handbrake
          -page 21

    (vi) steering
          -pages 15, 18, 22, 23, 34, 35, 45

5. Move away safely/under control.
    -pages 32, 40, 41, 63

6. Stop the vehicle in emergency/promptly/under control.
    -page 44

7. Reverse into a limited opening to the left/right under control/with due regard for other road users.
    -pages 64, 67, 68

8. Turn round by means of forward and reverse gears/ under control/with due regard for other road users.
    -page 66

9. Reverse parking exercise.
    -page 69

10. Make effective use of the mirrors well before signal-ling/changing direction/slowing down or stopping.
    -pages 32, 36, 48, 49, 74, 75, 114, 120, 149

11. Give signals/where necessary/correctly/in good time.
    -pages 36, 48, 49, 76, 77

12. Take prompt and appropriate action on all traffic signs/road markings/traffic-lights/signals given by traffic controllers/other road users.
    -pages 49, 73, 83, 86, 87

13. Exercise proper care in the use of speed.
    -pages 35, 72, 103, 115, 116, 123, 124

14. Make progress by driving at a speed appropriate to the road and traffic conditions/avoiding undue hesitation.
    -pages 42, 80, 139

15. Act properly at road junctions:

    (i) Regulate speed correctly on approach
         -pages 48, 49, 55, 58

    (ii) Take effective observation before emerging
         -pages 48, 49, 55, 56, 57, 58, 80

(iii) Position the vehicle correctly before turning right
-pages 48, 49, 50, 52, 84, 88, 89, 90, 91, 92

(iv) Position the vehicle correctly before turning left
-pages 48, 49, 51, 84, 89, 90, 91, 92

(v) Avoid cutting right-hand corners
-pages 50, 53

16. (i) Overtake other vehicles safely
-pages 97, 98, 99

(ii) Meet other vehicles safely
-pages 52, 59, 88, 108

(iii) Cross the path of other vehicles safely
-pages 53, 86, 87, 88

17. Position the vehicle correctly during normal driving.
-pages 34, 49, 78, 84, 85

18. Allow adequate clearance to stationary vehicles.
-pages 59, 116

19. Take appropriate action at pedestrian crossings.
-pages 93, 94, 95, 96

20. Select a safe position for normal stops.
-pages 36, 43, 65, 69

21. Show awareness and anticipation of the actions of:

(i) pedestrians
-pages 52, 54, 56, 78, 83, 104, 117, 118, 119

(ii) cyclists
-pages 60, 102, 104, 120, 121, 122

(iii) other drivers
-pages 78, 79, 81, 82, 83, 88, 102, 104, 108, 109, 110, 111, 112, 113

After the Test

Introduction

After passing your test you will have a licence which permits you to drive anywhere in the UK and almost anywhere in Europe.

Holidays and business appointments generally involve journeys where you will be driving on major roads for much greater distances and at faster speeds than you are used to. Take advantage of your instructor's experience and ask him or her to give you some practice driving at higher speeds before you take your test.

Although you cannot drive on motorways until you have passed your test, you can experience similar conditions on dual carriageways with national speed limits. Try to find one with motorway-type entrances and exits.

After passing your test, book another two-hour session so that your instructor can supervise your first motorway drive.

Before going out to practise you should first learn the Highway Code rules listed below. Next work through the lesson and finally complete the checkpoint.

Rule	48	Driving long distances.
Rules	71-73	Road markings.
Rules	84-92	Overtaking.
Rules	132-137	Breakdowns and accidents.
Rules	154-185	Motorways.
Rules	186-197	Level crossings.

Stage

10

How to reduce frustration and anxiety

Sometimes it seems that once things start to go wrong nothing seems to go right.

During a journey, the later you get, the more other people seem to be crawling. Everyone seems to get in your way and all the traffic lights seem to be on red. You get more frustrated and start feeling anxious.

Start your journey early. Starting in plenty of time will give you more opportunity to enjoy the journey and avoid some of the frustration and anxiety which is otherwise likely to build up due to hold-ups and diversions.

Once you find yourself late it will be more difficult to concentrate. The later you become the more risks you may be prepared to take.

A word must be said about the planning and timing of your journey as even the best laid plans can go wrong.

If this should happen and you find yourself behind schedule, remember that it is far better to arrive late and composed for an important meeting than to arrive flustered, or worse still not to arrive at all.

Before setting out on a long, unfamiliar journey plan the route and jot down the road numbers and towns along the way. Make a note of any motor-ways and exit numbers marked on the map. You will notice these on the bottom left-hand corner of the direction signs located just before the exits.

A route card only takes a few minutes to prepare and it reduces the need for in-car map reading, especially if you are on your own. Notes are easier to use for quick reference.

As you drive along, look out for major road numbers like the A1 and the name of the next big town on green signs (blue for motorway routes). This colour coding helps you to pick out the sign you want to read more easily. Less important routes and local direction signs have a white background.

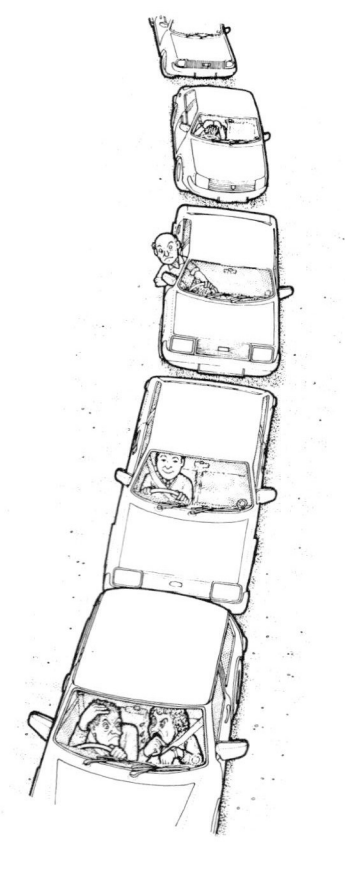

Lane discipline and motorway rules

After passing your test you are allowed to drive on motorways. To join one you usually approach from a slip road. Look for a safe gap in the traffic and accelerate until your speed matches that of the vehicles in the nearside lane. When travelling on motorways drive in the left lane. Use the middle and right-hand lanes for overtaking only.

Motorway driving means more things to think about. Look out for overtaking traffic. Use your mirrors frequently and avoid changing lanes unnecessarily. Let others overtake you or move into the lane ahead of you from slip roads, where motorways end and at lane diversions.

To leave, look for the exit signs and get into the left lane. Carry on to the next junction if you miss your turn.

Check your speed before reaching the end of the deceleration lane; you may be travelling faster than you think.

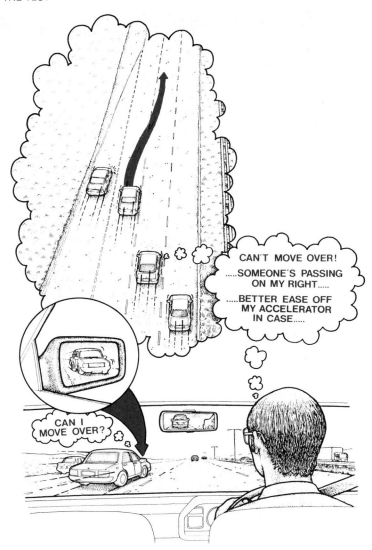

Stage

10

How to reduce the risk of a breakdown

Before the journey walk around your car and look for any obvious defects such as loose trims, number plates or exhausts hanging down. Make sure the car is maintained according to the manufacturer's recommendations by skilled mechanics. This will reduce your chances of breaking down or being involved in an accident as a result of mechanical failure.

If you should break down on the road, always think of others and try to get your vehicle off the main highway. If you are on a motorway get on to the hard shoulder and phone for help. If the emergency telephones are out of order stay with your vehicle and wait for the special police patrols.

Switch your hazard flashers on and erect a warning triangle if you have one. Do not attempt any major repairs at the roadside; if you need to carry out a minor repair think about your own safety and that of passing drivers.

The simple checks shown on the opposite page will help to lessen the chances of breaking down, having an accident or using your vehicle illegally.

Weekly vehicle checks

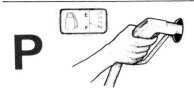

P

P is for petrol. Avoid driving with much less than a quarter tank of fuel. Check this at the start of a journey. Very few service stations are open late at night; even on trunk roads and motorways there may be long distances between service areas.

O

O is for oil. Check the engine oil and brake fluid. Look for tell-tale oil drips on your drive. If the oil pressure or brake warning lights come on, stop and get help.

W

W is for water. Top up the windscreen washer bottle. Check the radiator coolant level. Do this when the engine is cold. Removing the radiator cap when the engine is hot may result in scalding steam and water spraying over you.

E

E is for electrics. Check the lights and indicators are working. Carry spare bulbs in the car. These can be changed quickly at the roadside. Check that the electrolite level in the battery covers the tops of the plates. Top up with distilled water if necessary.

R

R is for rubber. Check the pressures when the tyres are cold. Check the tread depth and make sure there are no cuts or bulges in them. Check the spare tyre. Check the fan belt is tight and not frayed. Get the wiper blades replaced if they start smearing the windscreen.

Stage 10

How to change a wheel

Put the handbrake on, leave the car in gear and switch the hazard flasher on. Try to position the car on level, firm ground. If you are on a slope, position a brick or similar object close to each side of one of the other wheels to prevent movement. Keep an eye on the other traffic and take care not to stand in front of the lights at night.

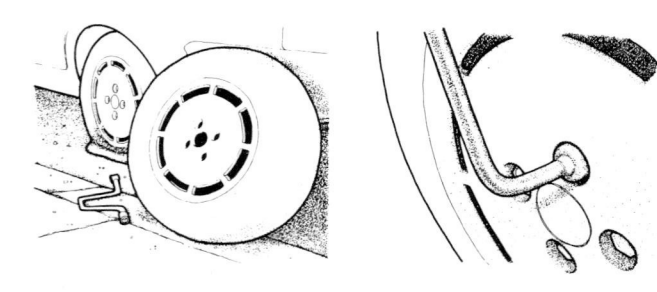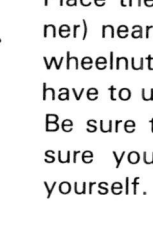

Place the spare wheel, jack and wheelbrace (spanner) near the tyre to be changed. First, loosen the wheelnuts slightly. If they are too tight you may have to use your foot and body-weight on the lever. Be sure to support yourself if doing this and make sure your foot does not slip or you may injure yourself.

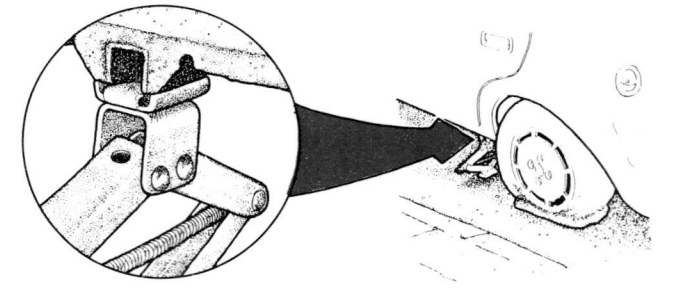

Position the jack under a solid part of the vehicle or locate it in the special jacking point shown in your car's handbook and then raise the vehicle.

The new tyre will need more ground clearance than the flat one. Allow for this when jacking up the vehicle. Remove the loosened nuts and take off the wheel.

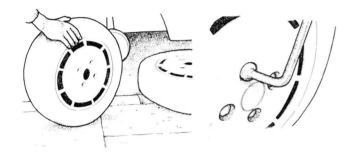

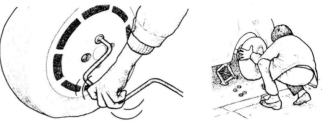

Fit the new wheel and put one of the nuts on finger tight. Fit the other nuts and tighten them lightly with the brace.

Lower the jack and tighten up the wheel nuts thoroughly. Check the pressure of the replacement tyre at the first opportunity.

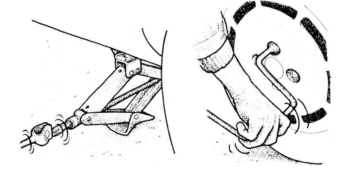

Remove the chocks and do not forget to put the tools away.

Stage 10

Checkpoint

1. If you become tired while driving should you:
[a] open a window?
[b] stop at a suitable place and rest?
[c] either [a] or [b]?

2. Areas of white diagonal stripes painted on the road are to:
[a] separate opposing streams of traffic.
[b] protect right-turning traffic.
[c] both [a] and [b].

3. Red reflective road studs will be found:
[a] along the right edge of the road.
[b] along the centre of the road.
[c] along the left edge of the road.

4. It is more difficult to judge speed and distance:
[a] in morning mist.
[b] at dusk.
[c] both [a] and [b].

5. Overtaking is permitted on the left:
[a] in one way streets.
[b] when turning left at a junction.
[c] both [a] and [b].

6. When in doubt would you:
[a] overtake cautiously?
[b] overtake quickly?
[c] not overtake?

7. You should not overtake:
[a] on two-lane highways.
[b] on dual carriageways.
[c] near junctions.

8. Overtaking is most dangerous:
[a] in a built-up area.
[b] on a country road.
[c] approaching a bend.

9. When joining a motorway, would you use the slip road to:
[a] build up your speed?
[b] look for a safe gap in the traffic?
[c] both [a] and [b]?

10. When joining a motorway, would you be travelling at:
[a] 40mph?
[b] 50mph?
[c] the same speed as traffic in the nearside lane?

11. Learner drivers must not:
[a] use motorways.
[b] overtake.
[c] use dual carriageways.

12. On a motorway, do you leave on the:
[a] left?
[b] right?
[c] left or right?

13. On a motorway, something falls from your vehicle, should you:
[a] stop on the hard shoulder and retrieve it?
[b] stop on the hard shoulder and phone the police?
[c] leave at the next exit and phone the police?

14. Flashing red lights above your lane mean:
[a] do not proceed any further in this lane.
[b] leave at the next exit.
[c] move into the next lane.

15. If your vehicle breaks down on a level crossing, would you first:
[a] push the vehicle clear?
[b] get your passengers out?
[c] phone the signalman?

16. Flashing red lights at level crossings mean:
[a] stop and wait.
[b] you have five seconds to cross.
[c] the gates will fall in five seconds.

17. If you break down should you first:

[a] phone for breakdown services?
[b] think of other traffic?
[c] get passengers out of the vehicle?

18. Anxiety and frustration can be reduced by:

[a] starting your journey earlier.
[b] keeping the car well ventilated.
[c] neither [a] nor [b].

Checkpoint answers

1. [c]   2. [c]   3. [c]   4. [c]   5. [c]   6. [c]

7. [c]   8. [c]   9. [c]   10. [c]   11. [a]   12. [a]

13. [b]   14. [a]   15. [b]   16. [a]   17. [b]   18. [a]